Wonders of Grooming

by Bonnie (Wonders) Trent

ISBN-13: 978-0-9790676-3-1

Acknowledgments

I would like to acknowledge my children, John and Jessica, who put up with many a customer dog being in the family bathtub when I was learning to groom. They survived a mother not being as attentive as some when I had spent too many hours at work. "Yes, see I do love you more than the dogs."

I thank Sally Liddick, who decided that I apparently had enough talent to ask me to write a column for *Groomer to Groomer* and eventually the making of this book.

To my husband David Trent, who all too often bears more of the "home-work" around here than he should, due to my various "projects." He is, without a doubt, my perfect match that had eluded me for so many years. A kinder, more giving man that I am blessed to have by my side each day.

To Max, that crayon-eating beast of a dog with a heart that would melt anybody. Also, the only Airedale that could pull off a "bikini" clip and wear it proudly. He is long gone, but never forgotten.

To those of you who have followed my adventures with the "Wonders of Grooming" column for so many years. I thank you from the bottom of my heart for letting me know that you enjoy the stories.

And of course to all the customers and friends who have had their names changed so that I might poke fun at their oddities without suing me!

God Bless you all.

Table of Contents

Chapter 1

Bow-nanza

I'm very good at coming up with great ideas. The only problem is that I'm usually the only one who thinks they're great. Take my stab at making bows for my grooming clients…

I went into a craft shop one day and saw these adorable flocked teddy bears. I knew these would look great in the middle of ribbons. However, I don't like to make bows, so I enlisted my mother.

"Mom, I have something for you to occupy your time, and you'll love it!" I announced.

"No, I don't need anything to 'occupy' my time!" was her less than enthusiastic response. "Make the kids do it," she added.

"But this is great for you. It's winter and you don't want to go outside anyhow, so this is something you can do where it's nice and warm," I said.

"I could be cooking. That's nice and warm, but you don't see me doing it now, do you?" she retorted. I was beginning to sense that she might not want to do this. I needed to say something that would just tug at her heart strings, so she couldn't refuse. After all, I'm the baby of the family, and I could play on her emotions.

"I'll pay you," I told her.

"What do you want done?" she smiled. And so she began making bows.

As any of you who have tried to make a simple bow know, they're not that simple. At our last count, we had 400 or so pathetic looking "things." I surveyed our pile of rejects.

"What are we supposed to do with all these?" I asked.

"Put the ugly ones on ugly dogs!" was her reply.

"I can't do that," I squealed. "These are awful!"

"Well, if you'd get me a decent crochet hook and bigger rubber bands, they wouldn't look like that!" she remarked.

Was it my imagination, or did she sound huffy? I didn't care for her tone of voice as I watched her feverishly cut ribbon. I decided to leave.

"If you need anything, call me," I instructed.

"Getting her to make some food would be nice!" I heard my dad shout from the other room. "She doesn't do anything but make those dumb bows. She won't cook. She won't clean. All she does is sit there with those things. I even have to run the sweeper for her. Do you know how many of those rubber bands I find all over the floor? And ribbon… there's little scraps of ribbon all over this house! She won't …" I closed the door quickly and made tracks for my car.

Days passed, and I figured it was safe to visit my parents again. I found Mom sitting in the same place I had left her some five days ago. There were boxes and bags everywhere, filled with perfect bows.

"I know how to make them now!" she said proudly. I must admit they were beautiful. "I'm getting sick of using these colors, though," she said.

"Let's try some out of lace, too," I suggested. I ran into town to see what I could find. I returned with bags full of many patterns, colors and sizes of lace.

"Oooohhh! This is nice," she said approvingly. "I need more rubber bands, though," she informed me.

"No problem," I said. "I'll bring them tomorrow," I added, as I started to leave.

"If you're bringing something, bring a maid!" Dad

yelled. "Mom hasn't been off that chair for days. She won't even make me a piece of toast. I have to..." Once again, I made a beeline for my car. Marathon runners were going to have nothing on me, as I'm sure I was setting records for dashing up the driveway.

It soon got to the point where I was gluing bears on bows every spare moment I had. We worked at an incredible pace. When we were all in the same room, it was total insanity, which incidentally runs in the family. Mom "bow-ed," I glued and Dad complained.

"Can I have a cracker? Maybe just a crumb of some old bread, if it's not too much trouble?" he asked.

"You can if you get it yourself," Mom would say. "I'm busy!"

We had literally thousands of bows. I stopped and looked at my parents. Mom, the "Mad Hatter of Bow-dom" was buried in piles of ribbon. She had that glazed look in her eyes...the kind I think rabid dogs must get when they're stricken. Dad, on the other hand, looked thinner and was badly in need of a shirt that didn't look like someone had shot at it.

"Maybe we should quit now," I announced.

"Quit? Quit what?" Mom asked.

"Making the bows," I said.

"Why? What do you mean, 'quit'? I know how to do it right, now. I can't quit. I can do them so fast, and they're so pretty. Look at this one, and this one, and over here," she said as she reached for the box big enough to hold Dad.

I was getting scared. She was truly a woman possessed, and I hadn't seen her so frantic in ages. I glanced at Dad, and he had a hopeful look on his face.

"Maybe you could just make some nice raisin cookies or bake a cake?" he said pensively. Mom glared.

"I don't want to bake! I'm happy with what I'm doing. I need more rubber bands, though. Get some different colored ribbon while you're at it. Don't buy anymore of this narrow lace, either," she stated. She was really losing it, and that insanity thing was worrying me.

"Just stop, Mom," I begged. I took the ribbon from her hands, and she reached out for it.

"Please! I want it back," she begged.

In one swoop, Dad dumped all the ribbon into a box. There was a glimmer of hope, mingled with triumph in his tired eyes.

"Oohh!" Mom cried. "My ribbons!" She reminded me of the witch melting in the *Wizard of Oz*. She looked up at Dad, and something seemed to change.

"You look different," she said. She glanced at the kitchen and moaned. "The floor needs cleaned," she said, as she glanced around. A flood of relief passed over me. She seemed to be getting a grip.

"I'm leaving," I said as I headed for the door.

Dad followed. "If you ever, ever get her involved in anymore of your 'great' ideas…"

"Legs, don't fail me now!" I prayed, as I bolted down the steps!

Chapter 2

Mama's Little Dumpling

"Remember - I want some of his hair for my scrapbook..!"

The first shop that I opened was a one-room deal. It was on the main street that ran through town. The front of the shop was almost entirely glass. Needless to say, I didn't have too much privacy. This, in some ways, was fine, as it drew many people to the building to watch me groom. Of course, this lead to many people becoming customers. On the other hand, it had a few drawbacks…

A lady stopped in one day to tell me of her Yorkshire Terrier, which she never had groomed. She had all the common questions plus some that, upon looking back, should have been a proverbial "red flag" to me. In my defense, I have a touch of color-blindness, which prevents me from distinguishing red from orange sometimes. Anyhow, she decided to give me a chance, and we made the appointment.

I suppose when the dog came in wearing a bandana over her head like an old woman with a babushka (Polish word), I should have taken the hint.

"She could get an earache if she doesn't wear this," the lady explained in answer to my curious look. She removed the bandana, and I thought I was going to go to work.

Sometimes you have to try extra hard to reassure people that you aren't going to put their dog's life in jeopardy. This was one of those times. The lady refused to give me her dog.

"She doesn't know you. She may become frightened," she said.

I just knew this was one of those "red flags" now. Stuff always happens to me. Steven King would have a ball with my life.

I smiled at the dog, mentally growled at the owner, and explained why she would have to let me have the dog. She finally consented to my taking the dog, but first made me promise not to hold her too tightly or drop her.

"She's very tiny," she said, "so she's very sensitive."

I very gently placed Misty on the table and told the lady when to come back for her.

"Oh, I can't leave her!" she cried "No!"

It only took one look at this woman's face to know she wasn't kidding. Being a new business at the time, I certainly couldn't afford to offend new clients, so I agreed to let her stay. I now know what the saying "gut feeling" means, as mine was begging for some *Maalox*.

I started to brush Misty and was instructed, "Not too hard. You might scratch her."

"I'll be very, very careful," I said, cheerfully.

"Make sure you are holding onto her. She mustn't fall off that platform," she cautioned.

"Table, Lady," I said to myself. "It's a table!" I was getting mildly annoyed.

I finished the brushing and went to the tub. This was the hardest part of the whole job. Misty's mother followed and was awestruck.

"You're not going to bathe her!" she squealed. "She may catch a chill!"

I think Misty's mommy was beginning to hyperventilate, as she seemed to be sucking in an awful lot of air. I tried to calm her by taking a new approach.

"Misty isn't just some dog. She is one of the family, right?" I tried. "She is more like a real person, and you take baths and feel much better. Imagine how relaxing this will be for her."

It was like talking to a child. In fact, I don't think I ever talked to my kids like that. It's always been one of those "Because I'm the mommy" lectures, or "It's this or reform school" reassurances. Anyhow, the lady put her hands on Misty's head, took a deep breath, and informed me that she was ready.

As I started to wet the dog, I noticed her owner couldn't take her hands off the dog's head.

"You'll have to move your hands," I told her.

"But you might get it wet!" she whined.

"I can't wash it if I don't get it wet," I countered.

"But you might get soap in her eyes," she offered.

"I won't get soap in her eyes, and it's non-tearing, anyhow," I retorted.

"What if you get water in her ears?" she puffed.

"Her ears will be perfectly fine," I stated.

"What if she swallows some water?" she winced.

"Maybe she's thirsty!" I huffed.

The woman consented to removing her hands from Misty's head, and I proceeded. The dog was behaving just beautifully. Why did the owner have to be such a hemorrhoid?

Suddenly, I hear something that really catches me off guard. To the exact tune of "Shortin' Bread," this woman was singing to Misty. "Mama's little dumpling sitting on a railroad track, sitting on a railroad track. Mama's little dumpling, sitting on a railroad track, but Mama and Daddy love her." This is no joke! I was totally astounded! And then she asked me to sing along!

This was it! I was totally fed up with this woman, and I could not contain it any longer. I was going to tell her to take her dog and all her neurotic tendencies, and go home! I gathered my courage, took a deep breath, and told her, "I'm afraid I can't sing anywhere nearly as well as you!" Boy, did I tell her or what?

The appointment dragged on, and I finally got Misty back onto the "platform" for drying.

"That air is too hot, isn't it?" she asked. I guess my look was enough to convey my answer.

When I was ready to tip her ears (Misty's, that is), you can imagine what kind of looks I received when I turned on the clipper.

"Be careful! Don't cut her! Watch, watch!" she said, and looked like she might faint.

Fine by me, I thought at this point. I really couldn't take much more of this lady!

Finally, I was through. I'd mention the part about the woman crying at the sound of each of Misty's toenails being clipped, but I don't feel it necessary. I was just extremely glad that this was over! The dog was fine, the owner was fine, and I was thinking of going back to office work!

My thoughts turned to what I was making for dinner, and of only one thing was I sure. I never wanted to have an apple dumpling for dessert again!

Chapter 3

Boo-Boo

"Isn't he beautiful?"
"Well... he sure is black!"

As I was growing up, my mother often said, "You should be a politician." She always said I could sugarcoat anything and have anyone believe it. So I followed her advice and became a groomer. Now before you get defensive, let me tell a true story to which I know you can all attest (I think!).

A new customer, who in order to protect the guilty we will call Mrs. Apple, calls for an appointment. In her *almost* exact words, she tells me the following. "Talk around the beauty shop, to which I am a frequent customer, is that you are very good. I have a simply gorgeous black poodle. He is AKC registered, and has a magnificent coat. I have been taking him to _____ for the last eight years, and I am not at all happy with what they're doing to my *Boo-Boo*. I think he deserves a haircut to bring out all his inner beauty. I trust you can do this for us?" She continued, "He's wonderful to groom, and is probably one of the most beautiful animals you will ever have the chance to work on."

I, at this point, am getting a feeling that my head is swelling to watermelon size, knowing that I'm famous at the beauty shop. I can do anything! I offer her an appointment at 10:00 a.m. on Tuesday.

"No good," she says. "My day to volunteer at the hospital."

"Wednesday at 9:30 a.m.?" I question.

"No, dear. Water aerobics, you see."

"Friday at 2:00 p.m.?" I tried.

"Oops! My hair appointment at..."

"The beauty shop?" I offered. "Why don't you give ME a choice of days?" I asked. "Maybe we can arrange something that way." We finally decide on a date and time that suits us both.

The fateful day arrives, and a car that was in no way related to a compact pulls up. Out steps a graceful looking older woman, with impeccable hair and a coat which I am almost positive was not purchased in *Woolworth's*. I watched anxiously as she opened the back door for the canine that would have won at *Westminster*, had he been entered. I was really looking forward to this! I opened the door in heightened anticipation.

"Here is my *Boo-Boo*!" announced Mrs. Apple, who positively beamed. Then a mighty *SPLAT* and groan, and there, certainly, was a "Boo-Boo!" A 35-pound poodle fell out the door. Panting heavily, he waddled over to the steps. I can't remember if I looked as shocked as I felt at that moment, or if I managed to fake admiration.

This dog was almost as wide as he was long! He had pulled chunks of hair from his backside, so that he resembled something in the gorilla family that I had once seen in a zoo. With almost three inches of hair growth where he did have hair, you could see straight through it, down to his skin. His teeth reminded me of what my kids carve out on the Halloween pumpkins, and I don't think he had one toenail that actually grew straight. But, he *was* black.

"Isn't he beautiful?" Mrs. Apple queried.

I do remember saying something to the effect that he sure was black.

"He is so graceful!" she said.

I replied, "He has such expressive eyes." I suddenly had a flash of *Boo-Boo*'s other groomer rolling under my desk in fits of evil laughter.

Just knowing I could make the best of an awkward situation, I listened patiently to my list of instructions that Mrs. Apple had written down for me. Shave him very short all over. She had drawn a pen mark on the paper to approximate a #10. He was going to look like a swine with that little hair on that fat body.

Don't paint his nails. Don't clip under the tail at all.

"What tail?" I thought. There was no tail. He would look like an explosion in the rear. Shave his neck extra short to show off his pretty collar. Like a #10 was going to leave long, flowing tresses anywhere else? Shave his feet to show off his fine bones. Sure, and draw all the more attention to those toenails that looked like Edward Scissorhands? Okay. I do what I'm told. It's her money and her dog!

I work. I am frustrated. I am disgusted. I am finished! Mrs. Apple opens the door anxiously, and I find out what the color ashen really is.

"You shaved him all over!" she exclaimed.

I am awestruck. Fumbling to collect an entire sentence, I apologize profusely, telling her I am sorry.

"I must have misunderstood," I said. "I thought you said short all over." I get her written instructions. Yes, it says short all over. I sigh.

"Well, yes, short everywhere, except the legs," she explained. And we all know the customer is ALWAYS right.

"Even though he's a bit heavy for a cut like this, he certainly is more beautiful than most other poodles, don't you think?" she said.

I mustered my biggest, brightest, most sincere smile and said, "He is one in a million, and sure is BLACK!"

As luck would have it, she made an appointment for six weeks away, and *Boo-Boo* now gets a "T & C" regularly. He doesn't have the density of hair to hold the pattern at all well, but Mrs. Apple is extremely happy each time and leaves me with a sizable tip for my efforts.

I guess the moral of the story is this: we all have many ways of hedging answers to questions that will offend our clients, but be careful of what you say in the name of truth, because you, too, will someday have a "*Boo-Boo*."

Chapter 4

Broom-Hilda

No profession is immune to practical jokes… at least not the way I see it. I do my best to spice up the grooming profession and none of my jokes have ever backfired…yet!

One of my favorite customers is a lady in her 70s with a heart of gold. We all have one or two of this type of client who makes us feel extra special. "Betty" must be Hallmark's biggest customer, as she never misses An occasion to send a card… i.e., Mother's Day, Easter, Valentine's, Christmas, Liposuction Day… Okay, so maybe not the last occasion, but I digress…

Betty always brings me a large bag of pretzels to get me slim, a larger bag of candy to make me fatter, and an apple to balance things out. A five-dollar tip is also included in every grooming, along with the comment that I don't charge enough. Her Christmas gifts are out of this world! The earth definitely needs more "Bettys!"

This does not come without a down side. However, Betty sometimes does and says things that make you wonder exactly how many bananas fell off her tree... if you get my drift.

Betty owns a mini Poodle named Mindy. Betty is an avid feeder of the birds in her backyard. Mindy is an avid eater of the birds that Betty feeds. When Betty catches Mindy trying to ax one of the little tweeters, Mindy gets beaned with a broom. I suspect Mindy doesn't really get a knock on the noggin', but the picture of almost 80-year-old Betty, running through the backyard (at .005 mph) with broom in hand does make me chuckle.

A while back I received a call from Betty. "Well, guess what that little dog found this morning?" she quizzed.

"A bird?" I guessed, with the utmost confidence.

"A snake!" Betty yelled. "A huge, awful snake! She came running into the pool room with it hanging from her mouth. I almost fainted, I tell you. I was screaming and running this way and that, and Mindy was running right behind me. She finally dropped it on my bedroom carpet. Right in my home!" Betty wailed.

"My gosh, that's terrible," I mused.

"Yes, it was slithering all over the place, and I was a nervous wreck," she said. "I stood on my bed for fifteen minutes or so until it crawled into my closet. I could just imagine it multiplying in one of my boots," she said.

"Oh, Betty, I don't think you have a mathematical snake," I said with a chuckle.

Betty failed to see any humor in my remark. "You know what I mean," she retorted.

"So what did you do then?" I queried.

"Oh, I was so upset," she whined. "I smacked it with the broom!"

I couldn't imagine her being that bold, as I pictured her dancing upon her bed. "Did you kill it?" I asked.

"Of course not!" she bellowed. "I was just so mad at her for bringing it into the house. What kind of question was that?" she asked in a huffy tone.

"Uh, I don't think we're talking about the same thing. You didn't use the broom on the snake, did you?" I asked quietly.

"Are you nuts?" she asked. "I wasn't going near that thing. I called the neighbor, and he took care of it."

"So you bonked the dog with the broom again?" I asked.

"Well, I kind of swept her fanny, actually," she sighed.

So, in view of her propriety and occasional eccentricity, I just couldn't help myself…

One day when Mindy came in from her appointment, Betty was commenting on the dog scratching. "She has been itching so much lately," Betty said.

"Maybe she picked up a flea," I suggested.

"A what?"

"A flea," I repeated.

"Are you suggesting I have insects in my home?" she said in disbelief. (You know how people can get when you say the "F" word!)

"She could have picked one up anywhere!" sometimes all it takes is just one to make a dog itch all over. Or, it could be just dry skin. Let's take a look," I suggested.

I know some of you will think I'm horrible for what next transpired, but I saw it as my big chance. I get so few of them that sometimes a girl just has to take risks. (It's kinda like the feeling you had when you stepped out of the car while it was still moving after that fight with your boyfriend. You had to do it, but who knew how much gravel in your knees could hurt?) Yeah, and that's a story in itself.

I put Mindy into the tub and started to bathe her. As I rinsed her, thousands of black things came into view in the bottom of the bathtub.

"What on earth are all those black specks?" she asked, horrified.

"They appear to be fleas," I offered.

Mortified, she grasped the side of the tub. "What? How on earth could she have gotten so many… where? Oh, my goodness, what will I do? Do you think they're in my home? Oh no, No! No! She was gasping now.

As I looked at her, she was peeking out from behind the door jamb and looking like groomers do when they overshoot an anal gland.

"Oh, Betty, I forgot that I used a walnut shampoo on Mindy. Those aren't fleas. They're crushed walnut shells,"

I said, thumping my hand on my forehead.

Betty moved menacingly toward me.

"You mean they're not really bugs? So she doesn't have fleas?" she asked, her eyes big as flying saucers.

"Nope. No fleas," I smiled. "Gotcha."

I was laughing so hard at this point that I didn't see the broom coming from around the corner, aimed at my head.

Retaliation can be a baadd thing!

Chapter 5

Bounty-ful Blessings

"Puppy left you a present outside!"

"My puppy needs a haircut… I think… I guess… Probably… Well, yes. Yes she does," was what I heard on my end of the phone.

"Okay, what kind of puppy is it?" I asked.

"A Lapapas Apsas," the lady replied proudly.

Yeah, I know. I was rolling my eyes too as I stifled my laughter. We've all heard some wild pronunciations of breeds. The AKC hasn't a clue what kind of dogs are really out there… (They think they're so smart).

"A Lhasa Apso?" I questioned.

"That's what I said," she replied.

Then I proceeded to the usual questions that I ask every new client. The conversation went something like this…

Me: Has it ever been professionally groomed before?

Her: Professionally whatted?

Me: Groomed…has it ever seen a groomer before?

Her: Well, I don't know. I don't know what a groomer looks like. She probably doesn't either. No. I don't think she's ever seen one. I could ask her.

Me: That's okay. We'll take a leap of faith on this one. Is she matted?

Her: No. She's spaded.

Me: (Heavy sigh) No. Not mated, matted!

Her: Huh?

Me: Does she have chunky gobs of hair that feel like big lumps?

Her: Oh! Yeah, she does have a couple of those.

Me: Is she fairly good-natured?

Her: Oh, gosh yes. Unless you make her mad. Then she might go after a piece of you. I mean I wouldn't turn my back for too long, if you know what I mean, she chuckled. She'll probably be real good for you, though. She'll just lay down the whole time.

I silently ran through the information in my mind and concluded the following: dog and owner have the same IQ.

The appointment is made and the "Puppy" arrives on its scheduled day. A hairball on legs comes through the door with the owner following close behind.

"Puppy left you a little something on your step out here," the owner said.

"No problem," I smile. I hand Puppy's owner a plastic bag.

"Oh, okay, I'll set it out here for you," she said.

I watched as she went out the door and bent down to pick up a rock. I admit this puzzled me. And I watched the woman do as she promised. She dropped the bag to the ground and placed the rock on it to anchor it in place. Without a heavy sigh, I know what's in store for me. I suddenly felt like Columbus venturing into uncharted territory. The owner walks back in and smiles.

"The bag is right by the poop."

I smile back. I bend down to get a closer look at "Puppy." He is unimpressed with me at this point, as he proceeds to lift his leg on the corner of my desk.

"Oh my, I guess he really needed to go, didn't he?" his owner said. My posture shrank as I headed to the back room to get paper towels. I return and clean up "Puppy Lake." It quickly brought to mind the time I brought home a poodle puppy, and he proceeded to anoint my husband's foot as he watched his football game. Don jumped into the air like football players do when they score a touchdown. Actually, the same thing happened when I brought home a second dog. My husband is now dubbed the official fire hydrant of the house. But I digress…

"Make him real pretty," the owner said. I glanced at Puppy. He looked the other way. Oh, I just knew how this day would proceed…

As I placed Puppy on the table, I noticed he really did have one of those Afro kinda things going on with his hair. All too vivid memories of one of my bad perms flashed through my mind. Yeah, Puppy and I had a lot in common. The only difference was I wasn't able to bite the hairdresser (or lift my leg on her). Too bad.

I began de-matting; the Puppy began snarling. I brushed, and Puppy pooped. I cleaned up, and he peed. I called the broker to buy stock in *Bounty*.

Our bathtub adventure was just that. Puppy was like a cork exploding from a wine bottle when I turned the water on. His theory was that if God had wanted dogs to get bathed, they would have been born with snorkels and loofas around their necks. My theory was that I had bills to pay. He would eventually see it my way.

The force dryer was a lesson in futility. You know, sometimes you just can't imagine how a dog can have that many bowel movements in an hour. Now I know I'm not the only one who's experienced what I call DPOW syndrome… That is "Dog Poop On Wall." Don't get me wrong; force dryers are wonderful, but they can be a "Loaded Weapon," so to speak, if used improperly. Sigh. More *Bounty*.

I scissored… Puppy growled. I clipped… Puppy snapped. I prayed… Puppy… Yeah, he did it again.

The door opened, and in came my daughter with one of her girlfriends. My offspring was beautifully dressed and ready to go on a job interview.

"Here," I said, handling her a small bag which I had knotted shut.

"What is it?" she asked, looking pleased. You know kids. They're always looking for freebies.

"Dog Poop," I said, nonchalantly.

"Oh… Gross!" she squealed with a horrified expression as she held the bag at arm's length. Her friend made a hasty retreat as Jess whirled around, beaning her friend in the side of the head with the bag. I smiled. See, you can make your kid pay for the time she told her teacher (one of your better customers) that you hate doing her breed of dog! Justice!!!

I finally finished the dog and tucked him comfortably into a roomy cage. He was content. I smiled. Another tough job well done, as I patted myself mentally on the back. Puppy's owner walked in, anxious to see what "Miracle" I had performed. As I walked into the crating area to retrieve Puppy, I held my breath as I peered into his cage. Ahhh... No doggy doo-doo. I guess he finally was empty.

I opened his cage door and let him run to his owner. She fastened him to his leash, made the typical fuss over him and paid the bill. As they left, I decided to check for mail. As I returned to the shop, I noticed a smell that was definitely related to Puppy. I scoured each room for a forgotten "token" of him, to no avail. As I turned to retrace my steps, I noticed that I would be able to do just that. I had forgotten to bag Puppy's outdoor gift and naturally had stepped right into it. It's amazing just how deep the tread is in a pair of Reeboks. You could hide half the population of Pennsylvania in them. Don't you sometimes wonder what possesses you to fall out of bed in the morning?

Gritting my teeth, I reached for the *Bounty* once again as the phone rang. It was my mother with her weekly report of the good sales at the grocery store.

"Paper towels are on sale this week," she was saying. "Do you need a roll?" I hung my head as I threw my shoes into the bathtub.

Chapter 6

Clipper Vac Heaven

Over a year ago, I moved my grooming shop to a bigger town. I had decided to go all out and get the "right" equipment, too. I don't think there is anything left with big price tags that I don't already have now. A few of the other groomers in town jokingly call me the "High-Tech" shop. Well, aside from all the payment books lined up on my wall, there is a higher price to pay...

When I first saw the *Clipper Vac* demonstrated at a seminar, I knew I had to have one. I was forewarned that it takes some getting used to, working with the suction. I knew, however, that I could do this. "It takes about a week," Marlene Romani stated. I would devote whatever it took to learning to use this, I thought. No problem...

We went to Indiana to pick up the unit, and I was so anxious to have it hooked up that my husband started on it that same day. We had a great time in all that installation togetherness. I admit that I am one of those instruction freaks, unlike men. You know how they do everything. They *never* need instructions. It shows they're weak. Kinda like asking for directions when you're hopelessly lost in the middle of nowhere.

"Is that tube thing straight?" I asked.

"Yup, it's right where it should be," he stated.

"Is the seal tight enough?" I queried.

"Don't wor-ry. It's perfectly sealed," he said.

"Isn't the box thing too far from the wall?" I questioned.

"That's not where it will be when I'm finished," he reassured. He was looking a little flushed at this point.

"Shouldn't you put the two tube things together before you...?" I know that look. When only one eyebrow goes up in a triangle, I quit while I'm ahead.

The installation went surprisingly well, even without my help, and I was ready. I didn't want to experiment on a customer's dog, so I enlisted our Airedale. *Max* is a very healthy dog, one of those that never needs to go to the vet for anything but shots. Hardly anyone ever sees him, so he was perfect for this job.

I started my new gizmo, and kept sucking in hair at all the wrong places. Poor *Max* lost part of the right side of his beard. Well, it was always dripping when he drank water anyhow. It would be better like this for awhile. I was anxious to try shaving feet, and hence *Max* ended up with two beautifully shaven poodle feet. This was easier than I thought.

I put on a #10 and shaved a rear leg. I skimmed the other with the same blade. (Okay, that part does take more practice!) I got a #4 and experimented with the suction. More, less, more, less. This was amazing! No hair flying everywhere. No mess to clean up. I love this. I read the instructions as I clipped. I skimmed *Max*'s skirt. Actually, I didn't do so well on that part. The skirt kind of got eaten off, but that takes more practice, I told you. I tried the whole assortment of blades on that dog. I did half of his back with a #10 against the hair, #15 with and against. I tried the #4 on the other half with and against. I was having a ball with my new toy, but it was getting late, and I was pooped. I laid my clippers down without disconnecting the vacuum. A hint at this point that the Romani's don't tell you: never, ever set it down next to a roll of ribbon. The speed at which it can suck it up is incredible. That old spool was flying! I shut off the *Clipper*

Vac and stood back to survey my creation. I have seen creative grooming, and this was REALLY creative! Poor *Max*. He really looked... Homely.

I decided to take him home and fix him up another day. When we came in the door, my husband was amazed. There was some remark about who did what to the dog, and why did he let "them?" I wasn't sure I liked his criticism of my grooming abilities.

"I'll fix it tomorrow," I said defensively. I was exhausted and decided to go to bed. I heard laughter coming from the living room and pulled the blankets over my head.

Morning came, and I found *Max* with a huge hematoma in his right ear. I called our regular vet, but he was away on a hunting trip in Canada. Desperate, I called several other vets until I found one who could take *Max*.

We arrived at the vet's, and I suddenly remembered *Max*'s haircut. I had been in such a hurry to get him there, that I hadn't realized how this would look! I, a professional groomer, new in town, new to this veterinarian, trying to gain new clients, and I walk in with "Freddy Krueger."

People looked. No, they stared!

"What kind of dog is that?" someone asked.

"Airedale," I said quietly.

"What happened to his hair," she asked.

Why are people so nosy? I wondered. I moved to a corner to wait.

People came in and out while I hid *Max* behind my knees as best as I could. They looked; they mumbled; they laughed! I cringed. Finally, we were called into the office. I had to parade that dog in front of all those people, and I even noticed some people hugging their pets tightly to them, as if *Max* had a fatal hair loss disease.

"What do we have here?" the vet said, smiling.

"Do you mean the breed, the haircut, or the medical problem?" I asked.

"Medical," he stated flatly.

I showed him the ear, and we decided it had come from our little dog's chewing on it. He decided to operate on the ear, and I thought I could at last escape.

"Your last name sounds so familiar," he said. "How have I heard of you?"

"I have a shop in town," I mumbled, speeding to the exit.

"What kind of shop?" he asked.

Gosh, why don't people mind their own business? I don't ask everybody else what THEY do for a living.

"Grooming," I answered, defensively.

"I see," he said in what sounded like disbelief to me.

I closed the door and explained everything, and we both laughed as I left.

Now that I know how to use the *Clipper Vac*, I can honestly say that I wouldn't be without it. It was a brilliant idea created by Marlene Romani, and it really does make grooming more enjoyable for me!

Chapter 7

Open Mouth... Insert Foot

"Since it's low tide, I brought my **water** spaniel for grooming."

Sometimes life's most embarrassing moments could be avoided if we used our brains a little more and our mouths a lot less. Sometimes we hurry along and stuff happens. I'd like to bring up a few pointers at this time.

We all make jokes about getting older and being forgetful. My mother says my problem is just that I have too much on my mind, and everything gets jumbled. I like her reasoning better than the age thing, but sometimes I wonder...

Take for example, the other day when I had a no-show. I was in a hurry, as I was planning to take off for a week. I was trying to stay on schedule, so I called all my remaining appointments to move them up an hour. I called Mrs. Smith to tell her she could come an hour earlier, if it was convenient for her. She agreed to bring *Chewy* at that time, as did all the other customers.

As I worked through the morning, a lady walked in with a young child and a Lhasa mix. The lady was holding the dog and staring at me, waiting for me to take the animal from her. It was obvious she thought she had an appointment that day.

"Uh-oh, did I forget something?" I asked.

"Well, we're here for our appointment," she said.

Oh, great, I thought. Another one of those people who just pops in when they feel like it and lies about having an appointment.

"What is your last name?" I asked.

"Smith," was her reply. "You just called me an hour ago and told me to come in earlier," she continued.

This lady did not look at all familiar to me.

"Well, what is your dog's name?" I asked suspiciously.

"*Chewy*," was her reply.

Ah hah! I knew something was fishy.

"No, it's not! *Chewy* is dead," I replied with an accusatory stare.

"What are you talking about? This *is Chewy*, and he's far from dead," she said, her eyes narrowing.

"Well, I distinctly remember when you called to tell me you had him put to sleep," I reminded her. "He had cancer," I informed her.

"I'm telling you he's not dead," she retorted.

"Is *Chewy* gonna die?" her son asked, looking up at her. "I don't want him to die," the child started sobbing.

"*Chewy* isn't dying," she said, giving me an "I hope you're happy" stare.

Suddenly it dawned on me that it really wasn't *Chewy*

who was dead. It was a dog named *Chaser*. Same last name... Smith. Different dog. Oh, I was embarrassed.

"Oops. You're right. *Chewy* isn't dead, and I did call you to come in earlier. Sorry 'bout that," I fumbled as I tried to explain my blunder.

Another of my more embarrassing moments occurred when I was grooming a Schnauzer who was very nervous. The dog kept relieving himself on the grooming table. I just knew the whole shop was stinking, but you know how you kind of get immune to a smell after a while. I kept bagging the stuff and putting it outside to get rid of at the end of the day. Every now and then I swore I could smell fresh dog poop. However, I couldn't find any that I had missed. At different times throughout the day, customers would give me a look of disgust as they dropped their pets off.

I continued grooming and close to the end of the day the phone rang, and I needed to make an appointment. I couldn't find my pen and reached for one in the pocket of my grooming apron. Oh no! Evidently one of the Schnauzer's deposits had rolled off the grooming table and into my pocket. I tell you they plan this stuff!

Here's a little tip for you... Never tell one of your best customers, who also happens to be a good friend, how rotten another customer's dog is. I mean, even *if* the dog is spoiled rotten and the people should have their heads examined for putting up with what this dog puts them through. Even *if* the dog doesn't look at all like what he is supposedly registered as. Even *if*, in your estimation, the people obviously paid far too much for the dog. You just might find out that the dog was bred by your best customer. Not that this happened to me! I'm just warning you to not bite your tongue too hard. Emergency room visits are expensive.

Last but not least would be this pearl of wisdom. If you are old enough to remember watching John Travolta in Saturday Night Fever, and the original Disco era...

Don't try to imitate those "Jive Talkin'" kinds of dances while you're in the shop waiting for your next dog to come through the front door. Sometimes the UPS man might come through the *back* door as you intently keep your eye on the parking lot. He just might reach out and tap you on the shoulder as you are in the "stretch your rear-end out with arms flailing frontward" position. You just might lose your balance and fall over a stool while careening unmercifully under your bathtub. All the while "Mr. Smartie Delivery Guy" might bust a gut in laughter. Oh, yeah... Stick 'em in those Buster Brown shorts and cute little brown socks, and they think they're Jay Leno. Personally, I love watching those UPS guys, and the stories I could tell! Ohhhh. The perfect topic for a future column...

Chapter 8

Poodle People

Poodle People. There is just no one else on earth like Poodle people. Well, except maybe Cocker people. Right up front, however, let me tell you now that I am a Poodle Person.

Okay, so just tell me why so many Poodle people want their dogs to look like every other breed except a Poodle. I've done Fi-Fi dogs that the owners wanted to be cut like the Isotoner puppy. Now, last time I saw the commercial, that was a Cocker puppy! But hey, they're paying, so skirts and feathers we make. (Have you ever really tried to make feathers on a Poodle? It ain't easy, Bub.)

I've had people ask for the legs to be shaved and the

bodies scissored (so they don't collect snowballs in the winter). They look like *Chia Pets* when they're done!

One time a man brought in a Poodle that is a regular here. "Gee, what happened to her topknot?" I questioned. Technically, there was one, but it didn't start until the middle of the dog's head.

"Well, the wife took one of those *Bic* shavers to it... It was hanging way down over Molly's eyes. She couldn't see," he explained.

"Good thing," I secretly thought. Then I wondered who it was that he meant couldn't see. His wife has pretty bad cataracts, but if I were the dog, I wouldn't have wanted to see her coming at *my* eyeballs with a razor. The topknot looked like a patch of wild turf growing in the middle of a bald man's head. Trying to make it blend in was gonna look like when those same bald guys do that comb over thing and think everyone thinks it look natural. Pretty sad it was.

"Just make it look more natural," the old man said.

"Uh huh," I replied.

Then there was the lady who wanted her Peke to look like a Poodle. "Uh... I really don't think it can be done with the kind of hair she has," I informed her.

"Why not?" she said with an attitude.

"Well, she doesn't have hair that stands up enough to cut like that. She doesn't have anything on top to make a top knot from," I explained.

"Well, can't you just give her a perm or something?" she insisted. "My friend has a Peke-A-Poo, and it looks just like a Poodle," she snorted.

"Well, to put it bluntly, you don't have any 'Poo' in your 'Peke,'" I offered.

"Some great dog groomer you are!" she retorted as she stomped out.

"Hey!" I called to her through the window. "You have a nice day, too! And don't let the door..." I secretly thought to myself.

Then there is the ever-expanding group of Cocker people who really wanted to be Poodle people in a future life. I have one lady who has a Cocker that she insists upon having a mustache and beard, not to mention a spiked topknot. "The kids mousse her spike and color her beard," she tells me.

"Of course," I smile.

Then there's the guy who never brushes his Cocker's legs, so he wants the legs shaved clean, but the skirt left long. The poor dog looks like she's wearing a tablecloth.

Then there are the cat people. They must have started out as mixed breeds of Cock-A-Poo people. I vividly remember doing a cat who had other ideas about where to spend her Saturday morning. A lady in her 90's brought in this flea infested 30-pound cat.

"I'll have to stay to help with her, I think," she informed me.

"That's fine," I told her. The cat was glaring at me while doing that "hiss thing" they do right before they make ribbons out of your arm. We put the cat into the bathtub, and as I started de-fleaing, she (the cat) started screaming. The cat started whipping around like a country line dancer who'd had one beer too many. The lady picked this precise time to let loose her grip on Fluffy, and like a ballerina way past her prime, swings her leg up onto the side of the bathtub, kicking me in the side in the process. As she hikes up her pant leg, she turns to me for a professional opinion.

"Do you figure these are flea bites?" she asks. Meanwhile, you have to understand that the cat is now zipping around the room like one of those giant flies that you try to kill while wildly swinging a towel, and you hit the ceiling fan and the light fixture falls to the floor, and your husband comes home and... oh, another story.

"So, are they flea bites?" I hear the lady asking.

"Well, uh, yeah. They look like it to me." I am trying to sound authoritative as the cat streaks past me and around the corner. I whirl around like one of those cartoon characters when something runs past them and screws them into the ground like a cyclone.

"Where's Fluffy?" the woman asks when she comes back to the present.

"I'm trying to catch her," I calmly tell the woman from the other room. In the meantime, I turn the corner in time to see the cat jumping into a huge trash can full of discarded hair from the Clipper Vac. I peer down into the depths of the garbage can, wondering how far down Fluffy actually is. Do I really want to reach down into that unknown mangle of dog hair? Nope. Do I really want to lose the use of my right or left arm (take your pick) as I try to locate this feline? Nope. Do I really want to get paid for all my efforts put into this appointment? Yep. In the meantime Fluffy's owner is calling to me.

"Miss... Miss... Could you help me get my leg down?" I run back into the grooming room, and low and behold, the woman still has her leg up on the side of the tub. "I seem to be stuck here," she said. And people think my life as a dog groomer isn't very fulfilling. Oh, if they only knew what I go through just to make my car payments.

As I help her get her leg off the tub, I explain where her beloved feline friend is.

"Well, I'm not sticking my hand in there," she says adamantly. "You do it," she directs.

"But, it's your cat," I protest sweetly.

"Yes, and it's my hand that I want to keep," she smiles.

I mull over all my options. There is one that is less hazardous to my body, but which will entail a lot more work. I choose the lesser of the two evils.

I carefully turn the trash can upside down while Fluffy's owner stands hunched over like a line backer at the end of the hall.

"Let 'er rip!" I heard her say.

Uneventfully, the cat ran straight to the woman. Thankful for the small miracle, I turn to retrieve the cat from the woman to rinse it.

"When you get her done, I was wondering if you could give her a nice hairstyle," the lady was saying.

"Like... what?" I queried.

"How about some of those fancy balls on her feet like that picture," she says as she points to the photo of a poodle. Sometimes grooming is a dirty word...

Chapter 9

Grooming is a Seven-Letter Word!

"We'll be happy to groom your cat, sir,
but first you need to go to a hospital emergency room
and have it removed from your face!"

I guess grooming is one of those foul seven-letter words my mother told me never to say. At least you would think that from the aversion some dogs have to coming here. Maybe it has something to do with the complex that the owners pass on to their animals long before they hit the grooming shop door. Does any of this sound even remotely familiar?...

Here comes Mrs. Baker with Gretta. As soon as they enter the shop (Gretta is the dog in this case!), Gretta starts clinging to her owner. As I reach for the dog, Mrs. Baker clings even tighter to her pooch. I feel like a lumberjack pulling on one of those two man saws. Naturally, Gretta plays the part of the saw. As I pull forward, the dog's owner pulls backward. Technically, at this point, Gretta starts looking like Gumby.

"You need to let go of your pooch," I tell Mrs. Baker.

"But she was looking forward to the ride in the car until I turned onto your street. Then we had to coax her out from under the seat with my son's Big Mac. She is so nervous. Ohhhh, I'm so sorry to be bringing you here," Mrs. Baker was apologizing to Gretta. "Mommy doesn't want to leave you in this place, but I have to."

Maybe I'm really off base with this, but if Gretta doesn't have a complex by now, I sure do! You would think I extract her toenails, rather than just clip them. This is the same customer who sends me Christmas cards each year signed "To my favorite groomer, with Loads of Love, Gretta." Yeah, Gretta loves me all right.

These dogs should be in politics. They really know how to play up the sympathy vote with their shaking when the owners drop them off. I have found the little rascals quivering with enough force to register on a Richter scale, while their masters are standing in the shop. Magically, when they hear their owner's car leave, the tremors stop, and they just look at me and grin. The grooming goes just fine, and when they hear their owner's car return, they once again turn into silly putty. The owner rushes in just in time to see their Jell-O on legs giving them a woeful look, and the pity party starts again. These dogs just eat it up. Go figure.

Then there are those owners who think that a leash is a

medieval constraint. They insist that their pet would never run away without one. Case in point… Here comes Brutus and his owner. The car drives up, and to the untrained eye, the dog looks happy. As the dog's owner opens his car door, I see Brutus squeeze between his owner's belly and the steering wheel (I must say it is a tight squeeze). Naturally free of any restraining device (leash), Brutus is gone with the proverbial wind.

I see Brutus make a hard left out of the parking lot while the owner is still trying to extricate himself from his vehicle. The owner looks right… he looks left… Suddenly, I see him take a quarterback approach as he does a menacing squat to catch the impending pooch. I know at this point that the dog has spotted the squirrel behind the man and is about to make a run for it. I smile as I see the dog's owner lunge left… then right… then left again. Suddenly I see the streak of fur zoom past his owner. From my vantage point, I can see "Mr." Brutus' mouth going a mile a minute. I am reminded of Yosemite Sam as I watch him whirling around, stomping on the sidewalk. This is all just too precious for words. Meanwhile, back in Brutus' world, the squirrel is now sitting high in the tree, snickering at
the dog.

Now it is my turn, as I calmly stride across the parking lot, slip lead in hand. While Brutus is giving "Rocky" a piece of his mind, Bullwinkle is hobbling down the sidewalk toward his pet. I reach the dog before the owner does, and I bend down to slip the lead over the pooch's head.

"Oh, he doesn't need a leash," the owner assured me. I smiled. "Just for this time, I think we'll try it my way," I said. Oh, well…

Then there are the people who are smart enough to bring the dog on a leash, but are looking the other way when the dog tries to make a mad dash for the neighbor's cat on the other side of the street. A basic rule of thumb here would be to know enough to pay attention to your animal so that your arms aren't extricated from their sockets when this happens. Only an observation.

The last group would be the slalom category. These are the dogs that could easily get a job on the water ski team at SeaWorld. They come in willingly till they hit the linoleum. Suddenly, the brakes are applied, and the owner just keeps walking. At this point you should have pylons on the floor for weaving in and out. Suddenly you spy the all too familiar trail of yellow. I dutifully make a sponge run, as it is very seldom that one of these Einsteins offers to wipe up the mess. And don't you just love how these owners totally ignore it? If you casually mention that Lake Erie is in the middle of the floor, they act as if they have no idea where it came from or what it is. It's the "it wasn't my child" syndrome.

I was at the dentist the other day, and as I waited for my turn, I heard a terrible screeching coming from down the hall. I hid one eye behind my magazine, as a lady was trying to bring her child into the waiting room. She was behind him, and he was doing one of those spread-eagle things in the doorway. She tried to push him into the office, but to no avail. The pitch of his screaming reminded me of a cat in heat.

Well, the dentist and me. At least I'm in the company of the Upper Class!

Chapter 10

Daycare

"I gave myself a haircut. It's okay, though. I practiced on Buster first."

Let me say right up front that I'm not anti-kid or anything. After all, I had two of them myself; and since I didn't bury them in the backyard or anywhere else, I still do. Not that they haven't given me great joy from time to time, but there have been other times that... well, you know. My point is that I know how kids can be and I realize how tough it can be to keep them in line sometimes! (Okay...most of the time!) There are just some times when these kids and their behavior just slay me. For instance...

There was the year that the daycare group from one of the local churches wanted to come to my shop to see what dog grooming was all about. The conversation went something like this.

"Mrs. Wonders?" a voice queries.

"Speaking," I reply.

"This is Miss Jones from the St. Peter's Day Care. I was wondering if it would be possible for me to bring the morning group of children to your business for an educational day?" she asked.

"I've had about all the education I can handle," I joked. "Ha ha," I added.

"Oh, yes… well, I meant the children's education," she said.

"I realize that," I said with my eyes rolling upward in Saint Peter's direction. "Well, I suppose so," I said. "You must understand, though, that I only have so much time allotted for each animal, so I don't have a lot of free time," I added.

"Oh… well, our daycare doesn't pay for our outings. How much would you charge?" Miss Jones asked.

"I meant 'free time,' as in 'spare time'," I told her. (This was one sharp cookie.)

I surveyed my appointment book and decided upon a day that would be suitable for the children to come visit the "World of Grooming."

I made sure that there would be a very calm dog in the shop for the kids to watch me work on. I watched the angelic little critters come through the door in an orderly line. I smiled. They had that familiar odor that I remember from my own childhood. No, not *that* odor! This was of crayons. I was instantly transported back to a time when my best grade school buddy and I were busy cutting out figures from construction paper. Never mind that the kid in the seat next to me was more interested in shoving the crayons up his nose! A classroom panic then ensued, as the teacher was trying to Heimlich him at that point. Now as I look back upon the incident, it dawns on me the Heimlich maneuver was probably totally inappropriate. My guess is that it beat the alternative of the teacher sticking her fingers up Jeffrey's nose to retrieve "sky blue and sienna," or whatever rainbow the kid had in his olfactory senses. My friend and I really didn't care. There's just nothing that smells as good as a *Crayola*.

I was instantly brought back from my Happy Place as a couple of these kids ran through the shop to find the dogs. I herded them into the right direction to meet "Stanley," a very calm Schnauzer.

"Ooohhh, aaahhh." The kids were so easily amazed as I started to brush him. We went through the typical questions about the dog, and I began explaining the grooming process. I felt like somebody famous for a while. However, that euphoria quickly changed to that of a masochist when I clipped Stanley's first toenail. I had forgotten what a big baby he was when it came to the nail trimming part. Boy, when the snap of the toenail clipper came down on his nail, he let out one of those hair raising screams that only a purebred Schnauzer can do.

Three of the kids dived under the other grooming table, while several others were bookin' under the bathtub like a herd of ground moles.

"You hurt him!" a little girl with pig tails was squealing at me. I suddenly had a strange sensation as I looked to my right in time to see one of these pre-pubescent monsters take hold of a shampoo gun. I, at that moment, felt like one of those water tube games at an amusement park. The kid was aiming the gun at my derriere and was hitting it with admirable accuracy. It should have been easy for him anyway, as the "target" area was certainly large enough. I should be walking more, I suppose.

I swiftly retrieved the shampoo gun from the little rodent's hands and at that moment, there was a mighty crack heard from the front of the grooming shop. I got out to the retail area in time to see a boy pulling on some of those anti-tangle springy leashes that were hanging on a display. The resounding *boing* as the snap end hit the wall was enough to make my filling fall from my molars. I turned and smiled.

"Oh honey, please don't do that because you might scare the doggy, okay?" I instructed him sweetly.

"So?" was his intellectual replay.

"Well, you don't like it when someone scares you, do you?"

"I don't care. I like being scared," he retorted. He gave me one of those upturned wrinkled nose kind of looks… reminiscent of a Shar-pei.

"Well, the dogs *do* care," I said, smiling through clenched teeth. "Besides, something might get broken out here. You don't want to get into trouble for that, do you? You'd have to pay for whatever you broke," I said.

"No, I wouldn't," he informed me.

"Oh, yes you would," I retorted.

"I don't got no money, lady," was his intellectual reply.

At this point I was wishing I had a shock collar at my disposal. I gently, (okay, maybe not so gently) grabbed the kid by the back of the hair and escorted him to rejoin the rest of his classmates. As I let go of his hair, he managed to get in a final stomp on my foot. Each of us has his own cross to bear, my mother always said. At this point, I was feeling as if mine were made from cement.

After various and assorted moments of more grief from this kid, the daycare's visit was finally over. With the walking typhoon's departure, I settled back into my normal routine. I retrieved a Cocker from the back room and picked up a slicker to begin brushing his coat. With the first pass through the dog's hair, I noticed the brush was dragging oddly. As I flipped it over, I noticed a pink blob of gum in the tines of the brush. I looked over to the rest of the brushes lying on the cart, and sure enough, each had a wad of *Bazooka* in the middle of it. I drew a mighty breath, as I tried to pull the gum from the brushes. Yeah, I was saying some of those words I was always told never to say.

Suddenly, I was interrupted by the ringing of the phone.

"Mrs. Wonders?" I was hearing. "Miss Jones here. I just wanted to thank you for your time this morning with the daycare children. They so enjoyed it. Perhaps we could do this again with the afternoon children sometime soon?"

"Oh, you're very welcome," I sputtered. "It certainly was an experience that I will be thinking about in the future," I managed to utter. As I hung up the phone, I wondered if the Devil's stomping ground ever really got that Cold???

Chapter 11

Bribery

Personally, my feeling is that a person can grow accustomed to many things, bribery being one of them. Take for instance, Butch, the miniature Schnauzer and his owner.

Several years ago, Butch and his owner came into the shop for their first grooming appointment. Until his first grooming by me, Butch had been clipped by his owners for years. In my own personal experience, the two most common reasons that pet owners do their own clipping fall into one of two categories: 1) They don't want to "waste" their money on "Fido's" haircut, or 2) Their precious canines have been refused by every other groomer in the Tri-State area.

In my case, the reasons mostly fall directly under the No. 2 category, or at least in a gray area somewhere therein.

Hence, this is where Butch comes in…

Let me say right from the start that the dog looked crabby to begin with. The owner didn't look much happier. But by the time it was all over, the three of us could have been mistaken for Siamese twins born in three's. (I guess that would be otherwise known as triplets.) Grrrr.

"How much is this gonna cost me?" he asked, glaring at me.

"Well, it depends on how much trouble I have," I replied. "Sometimes the dogs don't take to the whole process very well when they've never been professionally done," I added.

I quoted him a price that didn't include misbehavior or a flea bath.

"So, how much if you don't give him a bath? What if you don't cut his toenails, and I really don't think you need to cut him all over," he added.

I was spouting prices right and left. We eventually got to the point where the dog was basically coming in for just a visit. He dickered back and forth so much that it was like being on the "The Price is Wrong." His snide remarks were going to make the price of the original grooming soon double. He thought he was bargaining.

He finally opted for the works, and when he left, I fully understood why this dog hadn't been anybody's customer before. We definitely needed to break out the "face jewelry" for this one.

As the years passed, the dog became more and more difficult to groom, and the sentimental fool that I am, I became very fond of my body parts being intact at the end of each day.

Last year, Butch's grooming appointment happened to fall on Valentine's Day. At the start of the appointment, I informed the owner that "Butch" was just getting too much for me to handle. Regrettably, I told him that I was afraid I would have to make this his last grooming.

I was flooded with a feeling of relief at finally having told him that I could no longer do the dog. (You know how it is to dread seeing some of the clients come in.) When Butch's owner appeared to pick him up, he arrived with a five pound chocolate Valentine heart.

"Here," he said raising his eyebrows. "This is from Butch."

Yeah, I know what you're thinking, but how could I refuse to do the dog when my hips were crying out for a chocolate covered caramel? Yep, the way I see it, the way to a groomer's heart is definitely through her stomach. The only thing better is cold, hard cash. Now that really says "I Love You."

With each passing month, Butch became harder and harder to contend with. It was like being in the middle of a custody dispute where neither parent really wants the kid. Butch's owner would almost drop him out of the car window when he arrived here. I, on the other hand, would watch for the owner and run Butch out the door when I was finished. A kind of curb service, if you will. Once again, I found myself at the point of having to hang up my grooming shears with regard to this dog.

Summer was busy, as usual, and very hot that particular year. I received no gifts for the season, though Butch was coming in for haircuts more often than usual because of the heat. Butch and I were in serious need of relationship counseling. He would get testy, and the heat would make me short-tempered. He would retaliate after his grooming by pooping all through the drying cage. Those of you who have cage dryers know how hard it is to clean those big floor grates when they have used "Dog chow" smashed through them. My nose had permanent clothespin marks on it that year. I had cut through more than one muzzle strap while trying to hold down "Satan." My arms would look like I had been in one heck of a cat fight (which I had lost) after he would rake his nails down my arms. I was like his personal human emery board when it came to his pedicures.

The Fall leaves came and went, and autumn turned to winter. Christmas was fast approaching. The busy holiday season was in full swing, and I had decided once again to rid myself of the "Demon Dog." I rehearsed my speech over and over in my mind, for Butch's owner. I wouldn't back down. My resolve was unshakable, my decision firm. I would be like Mike Tyson or Muhammad Ali, whoever it was that would float like a butterfly and sting like a bee. I would be in my corner, standing my ground. I would deliver my decision to retire as Butch's groomer, and the bell would clang for my victory. The seemingly endless rounds with Butch would finally be over.

Butch and his owner walked through the door, and Mr. Butch handed me an envelope. "To the Best Groomer in the whole dog-gone world," it said. I gave my most affectionate smile to the beast who was busy lifting his leg on my desk as I removed the card from its envelope.

Tucked inside the doggy Christmas Card was a crisp new $50.00 bill! I'm thinking of marrying Butch…

Chapter 12

Help (Not) Wanted

"Has anyone seen the Chihuahua?"

Last week wasn't one of my finer time periods. I'm closed on Mondays, so I usually stop in to see one of my other groomer friends. I own and faithfully use a Clipper Vac, but for those times when I make even a tiny amount of hair on the floor from scissoring, I immediately clean it up. Not so with one of my grooming comrades.

I had stopped in to see her last week, and in the spirit of helpfulness and being a good "doo-be" and all that, I decided to clean up the hair on her floor, as she was extremely busy clipping a multitude of Cockers.

First, I guess I should tell you that I had picked up lunch for us at the local Chinese eatery. Chicken fried rice is about all Lou will eat in the line of Chinese cuisine. I will pretty much attempt anything, as long as it's not moving. Anyhow, I was feeling sorry for Lou, watching her work so hard, and I picked up the hose to her 900-gallon shop vac. Well, it might not hold quite that much, but it's one of those that look big enough to suck up a small cow.

"What are you doing?" she yelled over the roar of the vacuum.

"I'm gonna help you," I shouted back.

"But you don't..."

I couldn't hear anything else she was saying, as I feverishly moved the vacuum wand over her floor. I glanced up at her now and then and saw her shaking her head and waving her free arm like a TV evangelist, as she held onto the Cocker on the table.

You know how you eventually learn to ignore some people as they rant and rave about everything, but nothing in particular? Well, Lou is one of those.

"Whatever it is, don't sweat the small stuff!" I yelled at her. I ran the hose over the top of an empty work stand. I heard a nasty clickety-clackety kind of noise and shrugged my shoulders, as I looked questioningly over at my friend. She was pointing her shears toward her counter. In hindsight, maybe it was my head she was actually aiming for.

I turned my body to see what she was pointing at, and at that moment I knocked into a rack of books, which fell onto the chicken fried rice containers, which in turn, fell into a pair of Lou's new Nikes. I glanced out of the corner of my eye to see if she had seen the error of my ways. She had. Her teeny little tennies were covered with China Garden's special of the day. Ooooohhh, she was REALLY waving those scissors at me now.

I smiled and nodded my head as if in agreement of whatever it was she was saying. Actually, it looked as though she may have been swearing, but that's only a guess. I quickly vacuumed the rice out of her shoes, as I carefully avoided looking her way. The thought did cross my mind as to wonder exactly how long her socks would be smelling like Wong Foo's kitchen when she removed her footwear.

"Cha-chink," the sweeper said, as I zipped across the hair on the spare grooming table. Suddenly the sweeper shut off. I turned in time to see Lou holding the end of the plug.

"Why'd you do that?" I questioned.

"Look," she pointed. "You sucked up three or four bottles of nail polish, my Quick Stop is missing, and God only knows what else you made disappear!"

"Oh, we're exaggerating just a bit, don't you think?" I said, while fluttering my eyes at her.

"By the way, I saw what you did to my rice. Did it *all* fall on the floor?" she asked sarcastically.

"On the floor?" I thought secretly. She must not have seen it fall into her *shoes* on the floor. At least I was in the clear for that one. "Yeah, it all fell on the floor," I said casually. She'd never know any differently.

I glanced at the clock and decided it was time for me to get going. "I think your shop vac is full," I said. "I'll empty it for you before I go."

"Don't forget to get my nail polish out of there," she said. "And while you're at it, see if my Quick Stop is in there, too," she said with a tone in her voice that I really didn't care for.

As I pulled the hair out of the machine, I did indeed find the aforementioned items. In addition, I also located two grooming nooses, four bows, a small pack of latex bands, a face comb and a small pair of nose and ear scissors. On the other hand, I didn't find Mrs. Jackson's Yorkie that she has been missing for quite some time. Depending on how you look at it, that could really either be a plus or a minus. I hear the dog wasn't all that well behaved, so it probably is just as well. Ha ha!

At any rate, as Lou watched me pull her cherished items from the vacuum, her eyes got wider with each find.

"Do you want me to clean up...?"

I was rudely interrupted by her crow-like screeching. "Get out! Just go home and get out... P-L-E-A-S-E! Don't help me any more! Just go HOME!" she said rather unappreciatively.

"OK, OK," I said with disbelief in my voice. "I was just trying to help you out a little!"

"The next time I need your kind of help, I'll call the A-Team!" she sniped.

"Fine," I said. I went home and told my husband of my day's adventures, including my visit to Lou's.

"She was so ungrateful," I said. He smiled. He knows how we are.

The next day back at work, my phone was ringing as soon as I hit the door. It was Lou.

"Hey, what's up?" I asked.

"Well, you wouldn't believe what happened last night at my house," she was saying. Ready for some good gossip, I settled into my chair.

"Okay!" I said excitedly, as I propped my feet up on my desk. "What's your news?"

"Well, you'll never guess what my Danes did to my brand new tennis shoes! I came out to the sun porch to get them, and I couldn't find them anywhere," she said.

"How could you lose four Great Danes?" I asked, trying to sound dumb (which is generally not all that difficult for me).

"Not the dogs, you idiot. The shoes," she sighed.

"Oh," was my nonchalant reply. "So, get back to the story. What happened to your shoes?" I asked, in my best non-committal tone.

"Well, I looked high and low and finally found them in Ashley's crate," she stated.

"What did she do to them?" I queried.

A big sigh ensued. "Let's just say I now have the only pair of Nike slingbacks ever designed. I have no idea whatever possessed them to do that," she fumed.

"Gee... neither do I," I grinned.

Chapter 13

Seminars...

"I didn't know you had a Pit Poodle!"

There is a grooming seminar on accidents, and a portion of the program is devoted to accidents in the grooming shop.

I would like to share a few things about accidents. While mishaps to pets are covered, sometimes groomers are actually involved in the grooming process, but what the public is really clamoring to know is how you survive the other kinds of traumatic events. The ones that leave the groomer in a near convulsive state. In my case, the almost daily episodes.

I mean I could start my own series of seminars on how to groom after surviving trauma due to a lack of natural coordination. You know… the kind of hand-eye coordination that everyone is born with. I must have been in the bathroom when God was handing the stuff out, cause I have none. Zip…Zilch! ER can't hold a candle to my life when it comes to catastrophes.

There was the time that a dog escaped from his cage in my shop while waiting to go home. I was grooming another dog and noticed him streak past the doorway of the grooming room. A few seconds later he again zoomed past, headed in the opposite direction. Feeling something was slightly amiss (I'm so observant), I trotted out of the room after him. Looking high and low, I finally found him in the corner of the bathroom, crouched between the toilet and the wall. His teeth were bared and tartar encrusted. You know. The kind of stuff that is growing stuff upon stuff. It wasn't pretty!

Anyhow, he had a look that I didn't consider a good sign for my own personal safety. I'm funny that way. I have an aversion to getting gangrene or tetanus, whatever it is that makes your arm fall off if you get bitten by teeth that look like that.

I calmly fetched a slip lead from the back of the door. I probably looked like an ice fisherman to the dog now that I reflect upon the incident. There I was, standing on the top of the toilet, trying to loop the end of the lead around the dog's neck. There he was biting it every time I got close. Upon the fourth attempt, he grabbed onto the lead with his little vise jaws but didn't let go. The scene reminded me of when we lived in Florida, and you would see the guys from animal control snaring a crocodile from somebody's back yard. Yeah, those guys didn't have a clue as to what real power it takes to catch a wild animal. You'd see six of them trying to catch one lousy croc. I didn't see anybody coming to my rescue when I needed them. Oh, well. When the going gets tough… call your friendly (or not) dog groomer.

I pulled up on the lead and like a fish out of water, the little dog was swinging to and fro. It didn't take him long to notice his feet were no longer on earth. He immediately let go of the noose and dove behind the toilet again.

Once there, he showed his extensive upbringing in the area of house training. He peed on the water pipes that run into the back of the commode. Sigh. I know I write an awful lot about dog's bodily functions at my place, but there really is just something about me that necessitates their deep rooted desire to do it here. At any rate, I felt this plan wasn't working as I had envisioned.

I decided to try the towel over the head approach (over his, not mine). I should have tried this first, I realized, as I dropped the towel over his head and scooped him up. This worked amazingly well, up to the point where he bent his head down under the towel and located my right hand.

Suddenly, my plan went awry, and I was doing a Mambo kind of thing all over the back room. It was during this little dance that I tripped over the spare air conditioner and fell into the folding towel rack. Incidentally, that ended the rack's life as it knew it. It was folded really well, if you get my drift.

Perhaps I should have mentioned my problem with my weak ankles earlier in the story. I can fall over at the drop of a hat. I don't have to trip on anything or fall into a hole. I just walk and sometimes fall over… Yeah, I know.

Anyhow, as I lay on the floor, holding my left ankle with my left hand and shaking my bleeding right hand, the dog decided to go back into a cage all on his own. Do I really need to tell you that's where he stayed until his owner came to get him? I think not!

When the dog's owners came to pick him up, they naturally asked if their "Baby" was good. I tactfully informed them that Linda Blair's character in *The Exorcist* had a better temperament. They weren't impressed. That's okay. We, at least, had something in common.

The point is that the next day, I must self-proclaim,

I was a real trooper. I showed up for work with Ace bandages on both ankles and a right hand that was throbbing loudly enough to double as a metronome (well, to me it was audible!). But I persevered. A friend of mine who is a nurse looked at my hand that day and informed me that "Fang" had bitten into the muscles at the joints between my thumb and first finger. Being right-handed, this accounted for the stiffness when I tried to close the scissors as I was attempting to trim the hair from under a dog's paw the next day. As if I could possibly do any more damage to my body parts, I over extended my reach with the scissor tips and nearly amputated the tip of my little finger. I hear you!

Chapter 14

Out of Order...

"How many times have I asked you not to store the shampoo near the high velocity dryer?

It was the best of times... It was the worst of times. Okay. So it was only the worst of times.

I came to work last week and started working on the first customer. About midway through clipping the Poodle's back, my Clipper Vac shut off. I'll be the first to admit that I panic when a piece of equipment breaks. Yeah, I swore. Then I called my husband.

"He's not here," the airport manager said. "What do you mean not here?" I quizzed.

"Well, not here as in... NOT HERE," Sam clarified.

Now that I fully understood that, my next response

was as expected. "Well, go find him!... Please," I added as an afterthought.

I fussed and fumed, as I tried to continue clipping. It was like I had never clipped without the vacuum system. Hair was falling everywhere. If you knew how fanatic I am about hair lying around, you'd be more understanding. I'm just not used to it sticking to the inside of the tongues of my tennis shoes. It was beginning to look like I was wearing ear muffs on my feet.

As I was swallowing my seventh mouthful of dog hair, the phone rang. It was my husband.

"What seems to be the problem?" he asked.

"My Clipper Vac shut off," I wailed. "I can't work like this," I said. "I'm canceling the rest of the dogs!"

"Now, now," Don said. "You don't want to do that. It will just put you behind for the rest of the week. Besides, you don't want to make anyone mad by canceling at the last minute."

I knew better. He was thinking of the money that I would be missing out on. "You have no idea what it's like to groom without this thing," I said. "It's practically barbaric! I'll have to learn how to do it the old fashioned way. It will be like learning to groom all over again," I whined. "I can't work under these conditions," I said emphatically.

"Oh, come on," he said. "Aren't you going a bit overboard?" he asked with a "tisking" sound in his voice.

"A bit overboard? Is that what you just said?" I asked in disbelief. "Let me put it to you in a way that you can comprehend," I said in a grating tone. "If the screwer thing in your cordless screw driver suddenly died, and you had to run a hundred screws by hand in an hour, would you be upset?... If you had to drive 50 nails, and the head of your hammer fell off, and you had to pound the nails with a rock, would it irritate you?... If..."

"I get the picture," he said with an ounce of sympathy in his voice. "I'll be right over," he said curtly.

As I tried to finish the dog, the air conditioner suddenly shut off. Now what? I swore again. I flicked the on-off control back and forth. It didn't take long for smoke to start spiraling out the corner of the unit. It took even less time for me to grab the hose in the bathtub and douse the machine. However, it took quite a while for me to clean up the flood I created by doing that. The smoke stopped.

Don walked in just in time to see me mopping up the floor.

"Why is it so hot in here?" he asked. "Why don't you have the air on? And why is the wall paper all wet? Is that water leaking out of the air conditioner? What the heck did you do now?" he queried.

I guess I must have looked like the demon from within when I turned to look at him. He retreated to the back room like he had been bitten in the behind by a swarm of hornets.

"So, what's the problem with the Clipper Vac?" I asked, standing over him a few minutes later.

"You need new brushes," he said, matter of factly.

"Didn't you change them last year?" I asked.

"No... I thought you did it," he said.

"Now Dear, look at me. Do you think I have the *remotest* idea of how to do such a thing?" I asked in disbelief. Married sixteen years, and he still doesn't have a clue as to how many mechanical abilities I have. Here's a subtle clue. NONE!

"So, get me a set of new brushes," he said with his hand out. I picked up a slicker and handed it to him.

"These are the only brushes I know anything about," I said sweetly. "Some people don't do windows. I don't do greasy things," I informed him.

"Well, where do you keep them?" he asked impatiently.

"I don't keep them anywhere!" I said. "That's your department."

After he returned from the electric guy's place with the new brushes, I queried about the air conditioning unit.

"What's wrong with it?" I questioned.

"Looks like somebody doused it with water," he said flatly. "It's an electrical appliance, not a swimming pool. In short, it doesn't work," he said. UGH.

Don installed the new brushes, and the Clipper Vac was back to its old self. Never mind that I had to suffer with grooming the other dogs like they did back in the 1800s for awhile. I was glad to see the day come to a close.

The next day I came into the shop and turned on the computer. I went to the back to get a new stack of towels and took them into the grooming room. I flicked on the lights and nothing happened, but a tiny buzz and a dark flicker. No lights. I flipped the switch up and down to no avail. I walked out front to call my husband, and as I picked up the cordless phone and hit the "talk" button, I did not hear a dial tone. Slamming it into its cradle to recharge, I noticed that the computer monitor wasn't on. Again, I found myself flipping another switch. My trusty computer that I always complain about... with its mysteries of DOS was dead. I suddenly felt an empty spot in my heart. I missed him.

I sank to the floor with my head in my hands. I didn't know what I had done that was so wrong that I should be punished by massive equipment failures. I mean it's not that I couldn't think of anything that I had been doing wrong. It was just that I didn't know which thing was being singled out. There are many.

No lights. No phone. No monitor. No kidding. I went to the neighbor's house to call my husband.

As Sam answered the phone, I asked in as sweet a voice as I could muster if he knew of Don's whereabouts.

"Well, maybe I do... or maybe I don't. What's it worth to you?" he quizzed.

I gritted my teeth. "Could you please just...?"

"Yeah, yeah," he was saying. "Hey, Don, it's the old leash and choke collar," he was cackling.

I guess it was his best shot at humor. Yup. I was just rolling over that one. Hysterical fits of laughter.

"Now what?" were Don's first words to me. No "Hello, Sweetie." No "Good Morning, Skeeziks," as was his usual reply. Just that exasperated tone.

"It appears I'm having a slight problem," I told him.

"Clipper Vac quit?" he asked.

"Well, I'm not sure, seeing as how I have no lights with which to even FIND the thing!" I snapped.

"You mean the fluorescent lights? Did you try

changing the bulbs?" he asked.

At this point, my eyes were rolling like two bowling balls headed for the 3-10 split. "Do you realize there are eight, count 'em... EIGHT tubes in that one light! When is the last time you saw me have EIGHT spare fluorescent lights? How could I even get up there to see what I'm doing? It's pitch black in that room," I shouted at him.

In a far too calm tone came his reply, "Use a flashlight."

"I... uh... don't have one," I meekly replied. "That's not the worst of it. The monitor on the computer is out, and I'm at the neighbor's house using their phone. The cordless doesn't work," I wailed.

"When's the last time you charged it?" he asked.

Well, so one tiny thing was my fault.

I chatted with the neighbor lady until my husband arrived to take care of the day's catastrophes. As he pulled into the parking lot, I met him outside. I knew what he was going to say.

"Okay, it's my fault about the phone," I admitted. "The rest of it is just a fluke."

We went up the steps, and I yanked on the *normally* unlocked shop door.

I stared out the car window in silence, as we headed to the ER to have my dislocated shoulder put back into place.

Chapter 15

Retail Woes!

As I reflect back upon last Christmas, I vowed not to repeat my same mistakes this year.

It started out innocently enough. I had a major rush of the Christmas spirit by Thanksgiving. As we sat down to the "family feast," I was formulating my plan for something different for my customers. Something different for the shop, too. I would decorate like I had never decorated before. This year I would even get a tree for the place. I would make my doggie bags and hang them on the tree as ornaments. Lights would abound.

I would go into major hock buying Christmas merchandise to resell to all those customers who just couldn't resist splurging on Fido's gift during the Yuletide season. I hung mistletoe in the most obvious places... I was going to have fun at every good looking guy's expense if it killed them. Yeah, I'm married, but after all it was the season for being extra nice to everybody, right? Ohhh, I had the spirit all right.

I ordered and ordered. There wasn't a catalog that came to my place that I couldn't find something that I just knew would be a big seller. Naturally, I needed to supersede the minimum order amounts so that I wouldn't be stuck with the extra service charges. UPS was at my door daily. One particular day the driver stuck his head in the door before he started bringing in boxes.

"Does sixteen sound right?" he asked.

"Sixteen what?" was my quizzical reply.

"Boxes," he said with a heavy sigh.

"Oooooohhh… sixteen, huh? I don't know. I guess there could be that many. Well, bring them in," I smiled.

He wasn't kidding. I had been getting shipments almost every day since before Thanksgiving. If you people knew how small my shop is, you would know what sixteen more boxes did to my place. They weren't tiny packages, either.

A customer walked in before I had a chance to do anything with the delivery.

"Moving in or out?" he asked with a grin.

"Ahhh… a major replenishment project going on," I replied with a smile. "You'll just love the stuff I got. By the way, if I catch you buying toys at Wal-Mart instead of here, your grooming price gets raised 25 per cent."

"Fully understood and more than fair," was his good-natured reply.

"I thought so," I nodded in agreement.

Three days later between grooming dogs and the like, my place was bursting at the seams. I had the walls, counters, floor and windowsills full of merchandise and decorations. The tree was in the center of the bay window, fully laden with "Christmas-y" treat bags as the ornaments. Oh, making those bags was a story in itself. I recruited my husband to tear the decorative plastic wrap in appropriate sizes. I would then place the colorful gingerbread dog cookies, along with other festive holiday shaped goodies on the wrap. The whole thing was twisted and tied with ribbon to which a munchy rawhide was attached. We made 300 of these to cover the December customers and the holdovers into January first. There we sat at the kitchen table. My husband, myself and three poodles who were waiting for the cast off broken cookies that they were allowed to have by default.

"You're getting a little stingy with the plastic wrap," I informed my husband, as I held up a piece barely big enough to hold one cookie.

"Huh? Oh… I was looking at the TV," he said apologetically.

"When those *Baywatch* babes start dematting a cocker and bring you the money, then you can be looking at them. 'Til then, you'd best be a 'rippin' on that plastic."

"Yeah, yeah," was his reply.

"Sure," I thought to myself. "That'd be the day when Pamela Anderson would use one of those fingernails to poke an anal gland. I'd like to see her go to her manicurist then. Ha ha…"

At any rate, we finished all of our treat bags without incident. At least until I noticed we were one dog short in the kitchen. Calling Jackson (the dog) was to no avail. I looked into their bedroom, only to find him happily munching on rawhides and cookies. He had been stealing the finished bags and stockpiling them in his cage. He looked so content. We remedied that rather quickly.

I took my goodie bags into the shop the next day. Ohhh. It all looked so grand. Lights, tree, toys, fake wrapped presents everywhere. It had been a wonderful idea to make the place so Holiday-y… until the dogs started arriving, that is.

I think the first incident was when a German Shorthaired Pointer pulled a box of pigskin rolls off a shelf. Just for good measure, he then added a box of rawhide munchies and a tray of tennis balls that looked like my Uncle Sam. (They had faces painted on them and a single patch of hair growing out of the middle of their heads.) Far be it from me to chastise him at this jolly time of year. His owner smiled as he frolicked in the mess he had made. She smiled. I gritted my teeth.

After that, the next order of chaos was naturally the

christening of the Christmas tree. That tree had a male radar thing going on. It was like it beckoned these dogs from above, saying, "Here I am. Come pee on me!" I might as well have placed a fire hydrant on top of it in place of the angel. I thought I would have been able to avoid the problem by not using a real tree. This is precisely why I usually don't bother thinking. At least I know what my view is on the hotly debated topic of animal intelligence. Runs pretty much in the same vein as human male intelligence. There is none. Ha ha.

From there we ran the gamut of dogs unwrapping my fake presents to them eating the edible Christmas gifts placed on my desk by other customers. There's where I really draw the line. When it comes to food, it's all pretty simple. I don't share. I took down the names and vowed to bake them some Ex-Lax cookies next year.

All in all, I must say that Christmas itself was a wonderful season for me. Everyone was in a good mood, and I made out like a bandit once again with what I like to call "Prizes." It was the "After-Holiday" blues that worry me. Naturally, I reduced the remaining Christmas merchandise. Let's just say I hadn't had people flocking to the shop for the bargains. A lady was in the other day and was looking at some holiday collar covers, which had been a popular item.

"Well, isn't this just adorable?" she commented. "If I had known you had these, I would have picked some of them up as gifts."

"Well, these are the last of them, and of course, they're reduced now," I smiled, ready to ring up the sale.

"I really should buy some for next year's gifts," she said as she picked up several of them.

I held out my hand, ready for her to hand them to me.

"The problem is that I'd take them home and forget where I put them until next year," she said as she re-deposited them on the counter. I put my greedy little hand back into my grooming smock.

Then there was the lady who stopped in and commented on all the beautiful items that were left over.

"Oh, you certainly do have a variety of things, don't

you?" she remarked.

"I do my best," I said smiling.

"Well, let me run out to some other places, and if you have cheaper prices, I'll buy them from you," she informed me. Now we all think this kind of thing, but how many of us actually say it?

So as I sit here, looking at all the cheerfulness of the reds and greens, I am so looking forward to next year. Maybe instead of a physical tree, I'll just draw one on the wall. Far enough up that even those big dogs can't hike a leg that high. I'll let you know. Ho ho ho.

Chapter 16

The Move

"You're sure that's what you want?"

My shop has been in the same location for nearly ten years. I like the area. I know the neighbors. We all get along like family. Actually, we get along much better than that. Probably because we don't have to see each other on holidays or something. We don't give each other recycled fruit cakes or try to crochet one another foot warmers.

At any rate, it is because of the building that I have grown close to the plumber. Also, the electrician. It is such a pretty little place, but alas, I have grown tired of the floods, the melting fuse boxes and replacing motors in my equipment. I assume you get my drift.

Therefore, it is with mixed emotion that I will be moving to a new place. It is essentially brand new! This was going to be a great new adventure. So many of my customers have tried to talk me into opening a second shop for years. I have had no real desire to do so, considering all the headaches involved finding people to work there. I had also avoided opening an additional place because I didn't relish all the expense of doing so.

Merely moving my existing shop, however, would be different. I will be keeping the same customers seeing as how I am only moving a few blocks away. How much hassle and expense could it be?

I am now getting to be an authority on not being an authority. Maybe it's because I'm getting older that I'm getting so touchy. I fondly remember when I used to laugh when people called me "The Dog Lady." Yeah, I know, we all get that. I'm sure men get the same thing in the male version, of course. But now when I phone the man who owns the new place, I hear his workers yelling to him, "Hey, it's the 'Dog Woman'!"

These days, it sounds so different. It just doesn't have the same cutesy ring as "The Dog Lady." "Dog Woman." I sound like I should charge admission for people to get a glimpse of me. Just yesterday, I caught myself checking to see if I was sprouting any dew claws anywhere. Nothing so far. I'll keep you apprised, though.

Anyhow, back to the story. You would think I was moving to Korea with what this three-block move is costing me. Ideally, I could be having the time of my life in Bermuda (if only I could get over my story-in-itself fear of flying). I have written more checks in the last two weeks than I wrote in the entire last year. Checks for signs, for flyers, for new equipment, for more signs, for four color business cards. The last one alone even made the clerk at the printer's place let out a whistle. Somehow, you just don't think of a little extra splash of hot pink adding up to that much…ya know? Maybe next time I'll use a crayon.

The guy who designed the shop sign was great! There I was sitting in his shop while he worked his computer mouse like a maniac.

"I want hot colors," I said. "Really hot, like neon," I informed him.

"What you mean is fluorescent," he told me.

"Whatever," I replied. "I want it to really stand out!"

He drew this and that with his little tool (mouse). He added all neon — sorry, fluorescent… greens, and pinks and yellows. He kept changing the colors and writing styles and angles and everything. Each time I thought he was finished creating, I would say, "Ohhh… I like that… ohhh… that's neat! Wow, that's perfect!" He sat in silence the entire time and then suddenly looked at me and held his finger to his lips.

"Sorry," I said sheepishly. I glanced around to see if there was one of those signs that said something like, "Labor rate $50 an hour if you leave us alone, and a zillion dollars an hour if you sit here and keep saying, 'Ohhhhh.'" I couldn't find one. It occurred to me that seeing as how they make signs for a living, they should whip one up. In "neons," of course!

At any rate, the sign got finished. Hanging it was another matter. A twenty-two pound sign, they told me would cost $100 to hang.

"Look," I casually mentioned. "It's not like I'm asking you to hang it from the Empire State Building. It's only fifteen or twenty feet in the air!" I informed them.

"It's still a hundred bucks," the guy said.

Needless to say, I'll be hanging it with someone who will charge a more reasonable labor rate. My husband.

So, as the day of the Big "M" approaches, things are getting more hectic and a lot less orderly. Customers will be negotiating the maze of boxes out front this week. The dogs will love it, as it gives them more options on where to lift their leg when they enter. Up 'til now, they've had to settle for my desk or the door jamb. Ugh.

I've about reached my limit on stress this week. The

advertisement thing alone is about to kill me. I spoke to Sam Kohl of Aaronco about getting one of his fluorescent (neon, whatever) grooming signs. I had seen them before and really liked them. I ordered one.

I should have known that getting it out of the box was going to be an adventure in itself. When they ship those babies, I can attest to their being packed to withstand the UPS treatment. The day it arrived, I had three customers in here. Two were waiting to pick up and one to drop off. UPS arrived at the same time. The box with the sign in was completely open on one end. Trying to abide by the "rules" of damaged goods, I slipped the sign from the box, fully expecting it to be broken. As I pulled it out, I noticed that it was very securely attached to heavy cardboard to protect the front of the sign from breakage. Holding the corners of the cardboard packing material together were those industrial type staples, the kind that you can easily use in place of nails to build a house.

Naturally, being in a hurry, I ripped at the cardboard with all my might. In typical "me" fashion, I managed to get the wrapping off in one motion. I also ended up socking myself in the nose with my fist, and also raked the edge of the cardboard across my upper lip and cheek. At the same time I propelled myself backward with great force into the pegboard and practically impaled myself on some of those eight inch pegs on which collars were hanging. During my predicament, there stood the man who was dropping off his dog. He danced to and fro, helpless to do anything to come to my aid.

"Oh my. Ooooohhhh mmmyyy!!!" he was saying. The women just laughed.

Getting to the important stuff… the sign was in perfect shape. I don't know what hurt me more… the pegs in my back or my fat lip.

I have five days left before I am out of here… crisis to be continued…

Chapter 17

Feeling Faintly

Well, I am officially moved. Now that it is all over, I can honestly say it was definitely worth the effort. Also, I will soon be released from the mental therapy program. It was a total misunderstanding on the part of the police. They only thought I was trying to do bodily harm to my husband after he accidentally dropped one of the dryers. They never actually had any real PROOF. Hardly any bruises... a couple finger marks in his neck area. Big deal!

Anyhow, all went extremely well with the exception of

one minor customer glitch. There are good reasons I never decided to try nursing as a vocation, the following being a classic example:

It all started innocently enough. A long-time customer made an appointment for one of her Persians. Go ahead and call me a wimp, a baby, an idiot... it doesn't matter. As a general rule, I don't do cats. I guess I'm spoiled. I really don't care to work that hard. Give me a snapping, half-blind, nearly deaf, two-and-a-half-legged poodle any day over a hissy cat. Given the choice, I'll gladly take a dog bite over the skid marks a cat leaves down your arm if you aren't quick enough.

Yeah, I know you're supposed to put them in one of those cages or bags or something. I stay busy enough to satisfy me with dogs anyhow, so let me alone. It's *my* story.

The only reason I do the few cats that I do is because I really like the owners and I started them many moons ago.

Back to the story: The girl brings in the cat. This is one of those once a year deals where its hair is so matted, it feels like somebody accidentally dropped the cat in a cement mixer. Pretty solid from head to toe, it was.

Anyhow, the girl always stays to hang onto the cat while I peel it down like an orange. The customer is on the opposite side of the grooming table, doing a mighty fine job of restraining the half-naked hairball.

Suddenly, the owner's grip loosens on the cat, and she looks over at me. Her eyes were doing a fluttering kind of thing as she leaned on the table. "I don't feel so good," she was saying. "I feel kind of hot..." With her announcement made, she decided to let go of the cat and proceeded to a more comfortable spot... namely, the floor. As she started her downward slump, I dropped my clipper and grabbed at her. What a sight we were! The first part of the girl I could reach was the neck area of her sweatshirt. As she was passing out, there I was, hanging onto her shirt with both hands, trying to keep her from hitting her head on the tile floor. You have to picture me on one side of the table, practically lying on my stomach, while her sweatshirt did what all good sweatshirts will do when you hang onto a comatose-like person. It started to come up over her head as her arms flopped straight up into the air. Sensing I was losing my grip, I let go with one arm and flew around the front of the table in time to grab at her to keep her head from hitting the floor.

As I not so gracefully lowered her to the floor, I asked what every good rescuer person would ask: "Are you diabetic?" Where that came from I have no idea. What I would have done with the information is beyond me. It wasn't like I would have said, "If you are, that's okay, 'cause I have plenty of insulin syringes in my grooming cart." Being Bonnie Nightingale that I was, it just seemed a logical conversation to engage in with a nearly naked dog grooming client. You know. Sometimes you just have little incidents like that mixed in with your day to day strip down of cats.

At any rate, there she was, kind of in and out of consciousness, and then I asked her when she last ate. No, I wasn't going to make a run to Mickey D's. She did manage to mention that it was the day before since she had any food. The only thing I had in the shop to eat were cow's ears, rawhides and watermelon with cantaloupe, which one of my customers had thoughtfully brought in for me. I was really looking forward to my first taste of watermelon for the year. Did I mention it was SEEDLESS? I never buy that kind because I'm too cheap. What a treat it would have been! Deciding quickly, however, that the girl needed it more than I did at that point, I ran to fetch it from the fridge. I didn't bother to ask her if she preferred it over a succulent cow's ear. It was a judgment call on my part.

I got the fruit and was frantically searching for a fork. In this whole place I had ONE eating utensil. Yep, it was a fork, but do you think I could find it? Of course not. So, I ran into the grooming room, and she is still lying flat on her back in front of the tub. Bear in mind, we both have absolutely dander-covered, disgustingly filthy hands from the cat. "I can't find a fork. Let me help you wash your hands," I was saying. "It's okay," she moaned. She went after the fruit like I go after... (use your imagination) when it's been withheld from me for a month. It wasn't pretty.

I watched her devour all the cantaloupe, while she left the watermelon at the bottom. "I feel much better... Thank you," she was saying. As she handed me back the container. "I left you the watermelon. I wistfully looked at the perfectly cut seedless cubes. Did I really want to eat those juicy red, cat hair-laced chunks now? Somehow, they no longer seemed to have the same appeal that they once held. It didn't take me long to decide to pass.

The girl decided to rest for awhile before attempting to stand up, so I retrieved the cat from under the tub. (I finished the job by myself with no bloodshed on neither my nor the cat's part.)

I thought I handled the catastrophe quite well. Since that time, the lady has been in several times to purchase supplies. On her last visit here she informed me that she had been to her doctor's office, and she learned that she is pregnant. She offered that as a possible cause for her fainting spell.

Maybe we should all go back to a simpler time. I may change my pricing strategy. My new sign will read: "Will groom for seedless fruit(s)"... Take that as you wish.

Chapter 18

I Am Woman

"Can you make her look like this?"

I will be the first to admit… (Okay, maybe the "second") that sometimes my own popularity goes to my head. You know how it goes. One day you're getting messages left on your machine that say, "I just called to thank you for always being so nice to my Lucky. She always looks so beautiful when she comes from your place. I just wanted to let you know how much you're appreciated. That's all."

The next day you get an irate "Hey, Groomer Girlie…

I'm gonna sue your butt for the job you did on my dog. I paid you good money to groom him." (Like anyone else's money would be *bad*?) "You left his toenails on, and he scratched my new front door all to heck."

"And just how is that *my* fault?" you ask.

"I wanted you to take his toenails *off*, not cut them!" is his completely serious response. Yeah, my vet laughs, too.

One that really made me almost need a Depends was a long time customer who came into my new shop for the first time. A rather rotund little woman, she walked in with her dog in her arms and her son by her side.

"Ohhhh. How beeaauutifull this place is!" she was squealing. She thrust the dog at her son, and her hands flew to her little cheeks. "This is soooo wonderful! If anyone deserves a place like this, YOU DO! You work so hard and do such a wonderful job. We all just love you! I couldn't be happier for you. You have so much more room here, and it is so cheerful for you!"

She was reaching toward me with her arms extended wide to give me a hug. Going along with her wishes, I approached her and encircled her as she squeezed me in a vise-like grip. As we stood there embracing, she was what seemed near tears in her happiness for me.

"Oh, honey… I am just thrilled for you! Congratulations from the bottom of my heart!" Then a slight pause… "What is your name again? It is Bonnie, isn't it?"

Yep. I'm loved. Sigh.

A guy several years ago must have thought I was God-like when he brought in a severely matted cocker spaniel. He was one of those who wanted a firm price over the phone. Naturally, I told him I'd have to see the dog first to even ballpark the price. So, he brings in this thing with ears you could have made slippers out of.

"Wow, she's really matted," I commented. I gave him an approximate price range.

"Are you sure she's really matted. I mean for SURE?" he questioned.

"Of course… just feel her body deep down," I told him, feeling her sides. A big smile crossed his face.

"Thank you so much," he was saying. "I gotta tell my wife. Hey, Barb," he yelled out the door. "The groomer lady says Misty's gonna have pups. Rusty must'a caught her last week. You're gonna be a Gramma!"

I slapped my forehead with my fist... (I should have thumped his on HIS!)

"No... I said *matted*... not *mated*." He looked totally dumbfounded (hard to believe, huh?).

"What's the difference?" he asked. I explained. He looked slightly embarrassed.

As he reached for the door I interrupted. "Allow me," I said. I stuck my head out the door in his wife's direction. "Forget it, Barb," I said, calmly shaking my head. She looked so disappointed. The Amazing Kreskin I ain't.

Then there was the time the lady brought me an afghan hound and two boxes of "Pro-Perm." It seems she was tired of the straight look on her dog and decided that I had the ability to give her dog a "wave."

"I was going to attempt it myself," she told me, "but the box says 'Professional Formula,' so I decided I'd better leave it up to you."

"Thanks, but NO thanks," was my reply in a nutshell. I use the term nutshell loosely and in more ways than one.

There is also the guy who has a miniature poodle with an under-bite that any respectable Lhasa would kill for. These people think I am Saint Bonnie when it comes to clipping their dog. On one end of the grooming spectrum you have the people who want no more than 1/64 of an inch taken off the ends of the hair... then you have one like this guy.

Don't get me wrong. He and his wife are a couple of the sweetest customers I have, and their dog is great! However, they like the dong done with a #10 body, #30 feet and face. This is during the winter. She gets done every three weeks. Each year in the summer I get the same request for the last ten years.

"Now that it's getting hot out, cut her short. She doesn't need all that hair this time of year." So, I do a #15 on the body... every two weeks. They are tickled to death. Then they say everyone wants to know who clips their dog.

Sometimes I think it's amazing that I get any new customers at all when I have to do things like that. Oh, well. The customer is always right. Right?... Right!!!

Last, but certainly not least is one man that I recall as if it were yesterday. I get this phone call for a grooming appointment on a poodle mix. A six year old dog that had never been professionally done. He tells me what a great dog this is, and I make him an appointment.

He arrived on time on the chosen day. He is pulling an animal behind him as if it is going to the slaughter house (typical reaction). They can sense a groomer a mile away. Even though a dog has never been to one of us, they Still know what's going to happen.

At any rate, when the dog finally makes it through the door, I see hair on him that I really can't identify. It is a dull orange color with small sticky mats everywhere. The odor was that of a moldy-doggy-rancid-road kill kind of fragrance. It wasn't exactly reminiscent of Stetson or CK One.

"What is wrong with his hair?" I asked as I bent over the dog. I wrinkled my nose as the dog wrinkled his lip.

"Well," the man drawled… "He got in a fight with a Skunk a while back."

"Obviously, the skunk won," I nodded. "But, there is something stuck all over his hair," I clarified.

"Oh, that would be the tomato juice we poured on him. It's supposed to get rid of the skunk smell," he informed me.

Fully understanding now, but not necessarily believing, I asked the all too apparent. "You mean you poured the juice on him but didn't rinse it out?"

"Yeah, the vet told me to put it on him. He didn't say nothin' about washing it out," he defended himself.

Silently guessing that I really shouldn't ask the next question, but with curiosity getting the best of me, I did. "How long ago was this?"

"Oh, I guess it's been a couple weeks, anyhow," he said, matter of factly.

I love my job!

Chapter 19

The Dog Show

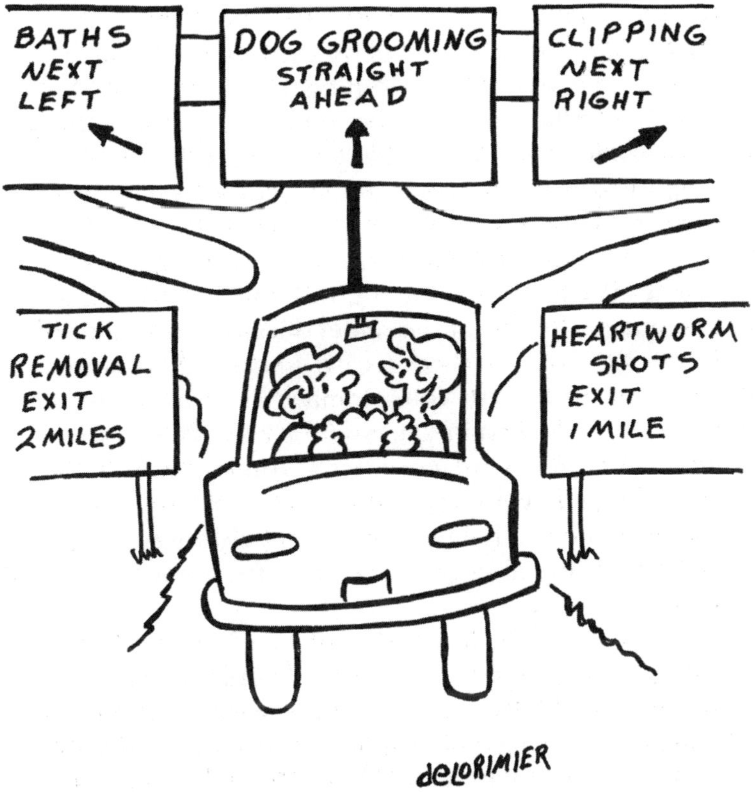

"I think our doggie will like this trip."

As in the case of many of you fellow groomers, I am involved in the sport of obedience (sometimes the lack of it!). There is nothing to compare to the thrill of being able to get away from work for the weekend in order to spend two days surrounded by hundreds of dogs! My family just shakes their heads.

I have missed several family reunions, birthdays and even my nephew's wedding because of a dog show. There really isn't much to compare with the joy of showing your dog. I ask you…what else could you do that costs you $64.00 for entry fees, $150.00 for motels, $80.00 for food, $30.00 for gas and places astronomical mileage on your car for the joy of 5 minutes in the ring? It's even more gratifying when you don't qualify for that needed score.

I pack like I'm going to fall off the face of the earth for awhile. Not so much in clothing, mind you, but in medicinal supplies. There is the Immodium to stop things up in case nerves get the best of you and Mylanta for the acid indigestion that occasionally surfaces when so and so can't help but tell the whole world about THEIR score. I bring aspirin to help ease the thumping head that comes because the church group that is partying in the room next to mine at the motel doesn't disband until 4:00 a.m.! Tylenol is packed in case your head hurts from the previous group, but your stomach hurts because the Mylanta hasn't kicked in yet. And for gosh sakes, don't forget the Metamucil, in case…well, you know. Actually the only things I ever use are the Tylenol and Mylanta. The rest seems to be needed by fellow competitors at one point or another. Best to always be prepared for the whole gamut is my motto.

Then there are the few fortunate ones who don't let anything bother them for very long. People who get the show jitters really bad are usually pretty calm after a short disappearance. I asked an acquaintance's husband where his wife went, as it was almost her turn in the ring. "In the bathroom throwing up," he replied, not even glancing up from his crossword puzzle. Ten minutes later she was trotting down the aisle with her dog, looking happy as a clam.

I recall the point at which my husband and I decided that it would be much easier to look into purchasing a motor home for our weekend trips. Many of our friends have them, and it was so nice to be able to go and relax between classes without having to drive to a motel and be imprisoned in a little room. It would also be simpler to take two to four dogs at any given time.

After much searching for the perfect tenement on wheels, we decided that perhaps $80,000 (and up) was just a tad more than we wanted to spend on weekend accommodations. Naturally, we went with a used model.

We purchased a 1983, 29-footer that has all kinds of perks, is cheerful, and in immaculate condition. We got it at the end of the season, so we parked it off the side of the driveway and promptly covered it with a silver 80 ft. tarp. (Yeah, a little overkill on the size of the tarp!) I remember when my daughter pulled into the driveway and flew into the house.

"What is that big silver 'THING'?" she asked.

"A motor home," I informed her.

"Oh," she replied, unimpressed. "It looks like a big bubble," she shrugged. Hence, we no longer call it a M/H. It has been dubbed "The Bubble" for three years now.

Anyhow, how wonderful it is to have it. I remember our first trip like it was yesterday (so does my Hubby!). We pulled out of the driveway, and Don ran over our garbage can! Never mind...we were on an adventure! We stopped to have the propane tank filled. I recalled in the RV book that you were never to fill the tank all the way, but allow for expansion of the gas or something. Needless to say I smelled propane for four hours down the turnpike. Naturally, the guy at the gas place overfilled the dumb thing. I was in a panic the whole trip. When we pulled into the Fairgrounds where the dog show was being held, the people around us were looking to see where the horrendous smell was coming from. Don announced that he was going to light the pilot light for the water heater. I literally ran to the other side of the grounds, yelling over my shoulder, "You know you're gonna blow us all to kingdom come!" Obviously, I was wrong.

After the gas problem was taken care of, we had a wonderful time. THAT day. The next day brought some rain. We had been down in one of the buildings doing our "Show Thing," and decided to go up to the Bubble for some lunch. We dashed through a downpour, and as I opened the door to our "home," I kicked my shoes off. As

I stepped onto the carpet in my socks, I noticed a rather cold, wet sensation overcome me. I seemed to be standing in water that was rather deep in front of the couch.

While I was squealing, I looked up at the ceiling to see where the leak was coming from. Dry white panels looked back at me. I sat on the couch to get my feet off the wet carpeting and promptly got a soaked rear end. I jumped up as my husband stood on the step, looking in.

"Why are you all wet?" he asked.

"Gee, I didn't realize I was," I replied, acting my blondest. "Maybe it's because your BARGAIN MOTOR HOME leaks!" I yelled. As we stood there, I heard a hissing sound behind me. It was coming from under the seating area. I pulled the front off the couch and was promptly doused by a sharp stream of ice-cold water. We discovered that not ONLY did the water heater leak, but that it apparently didn't heat very well either.

As Don went out to turn off the water, I used every available towel to soak up the flood on the carpet. Realizing I wasn't getting very far, I decided the only way to get rid of the water was to squeegee it. However, in my hurry to all the stomach ailment medicines ready for our travels, I foolishly neglected to pack the all-important squeegee.

I located the only thing I could think of. I handed my husband a small cake pan and proceeded to push water through the carpet with a pancake turner into his awaiting pan at the bottom of the step. Of course, this wouldn't have been complete without my whining about my freezing feet.

I remember well the look we got from the neighboring motor homes. They laughed. I didn't!

After getting eight or nine pans of water out of the rug, I turned to the next logical solution…the hair dryer. This, of course, didn't last too long, as the smell of the overheated hair dryer filled the air.

We left the carpet to dry naturally. I might add that it took the rest of the weekend to accomplish that. (I went through a lot of socks!)

At the end of our getaway, we proceeded to pack

things for the return trip. There are many things you must do before you can just drive away, i.e… Make sure the entrance ramp is folded away, disconnect the electric supply, the gas supply and the water supply (gee, that was done two days ago) and close and lock all the compartment doors.

With everything now put in its place, we left for home. As we passed under a group of trees along the road leading from the park, I saw a twisted clump of metal fall onto the hood of the vehicle.

"Did you happen to remember to wind down the antenna?" I casually asked my husband.

No response…

Chapter 20

The Internet

"... And then I've got a 'drooler' at 2:30."

I finally decided to succumb to the Internet... It wasn't an easy decision. I still don't understand my computer... It's only been eleven years! Give me time!

At any rate, I took the plunge. I kept getting those disks in the mail for AOL. They kept sending them, and I kept pitching them. Like I don't have enough to do without getting tied up on that stuff.

The other night I found one lone disk that hadn't quite made it to the trashcan. Curiosity overcame me, and I popped it into my computer. It all seemed so simple. Just follow the instructions on the screen...I did...IT didn't.

After a quick phone call to a computer half-whiz, (my son), I learned that, like me, my machine was too old to keep up.

"You're *way* outdated," he told me. Where have I heard that before, I wondered??? "You're the one who always said 'No way,' when it comes to the Big 'I'," he said.

"I was just playing," I said.

"You could update your modem," he said.

"My modem doesn't want to be updated," I told him. "Just forget it, I was just killing some spare time," I said.

I called another friend of mine and asked his opinion of why I couldn't get online.

"How old is your computer?" was his first question.

When I told him, he couldn't seem to get past its age.

"It's not like it's dog years or anything!" I defended.

"Dog years would be young in comparison to what you've got!" he spouted.

"Forget it! I don't really care," I quipped.

Naturally, being me, I was now on a mad search to get on line. Being told I couldn't, meant that I HAD TO.

Rather than purchase a second computer for the house, I went to Sears and learned of Web TV. For $250 I could accomplish my whim, as opposed to $1000 for a new computer. Armed with this new knowledge, I was empowered. With my new boxes under my arm, I was on my way out of the mall…

I knew I wouldn't have too much time to devote to this Internet thing… I never have time to do the necessary things around the house after a day of grooming, so I knew this Web thing would be a seldom-used item. Just had to catch up to the rest of the world, though… I needed to become a 00's babe (90's would have sounded better there.)

At any rate, I got the thing hooked up the first night. Read a few instructions…ok, a lot. I'm a stick-to-the-rules kind of person, generally speaking. When the eighteen-page agreement came onto the screen, I read each and every page. My husband looked at me somewhere around page five and asked, "You're not going to read all of it, are you?"

"Yes, I am," I said, calmly. He shook his head and

retreated upstairs. "And which of us is the one who never stops for directions until we're hopelessly lost in the middle of Afghanistan...?" My words were lost, as the upstairs TV's volume edged higher and higher.

After reading all of the agreement, I decide to spend twenty or thirty minutes trying out my new toy. This was 6:45 p.m. By accident, and believe me, with me, *everything* is an accident, I stumbled into a spot that seemed intriguing. Suddenly, I was "there." Lo and behold, in the name of all things good and great, I discovered a groomer's Chat Room... Whoooooo... This was something I knew about. Imagine!! Grooming and Chatting. Two things that I was pretty good at. All in the same sentence.

I met several very nice people, including one whose name is "Rev." The conversation turned to one that groomers everywhere can relate to... Dog slobber. Some might call it drool, slime, squealers, stringers...Call it what you want. It all boils down to dog spit. Anyhow, my story was one of what gross thing happened to me a couple of weeks ago.

"There I was," I told Rev. "I was thinning out the chest of a Golden and had my head turned sideways. My hair was pulled back. All of a sudden this big string of slobber fell out of his mouth into my ear! It was soooooo gross! I was dancin' around the grooming room holding my head the opposite way like when you get water in your ear from swimming. I kept squealing and this dog was looking at me with HIS head turned sideways. Bet he wouldn't have liked it if I'da spit in his otic cavity!"

"Ugh...that's disgusting," was her approximate reply.

Awful as it sounds, it did happen. I guess I've had worse.

Then, the issue of pugs and lhasas and those snubby-nosed breeds came up.

"What about when they sneeze right in your face?" was her casual remark.

"Actually, it always seems to happen to me when I'm 7/8" from their face," I thought. You know when you have a ton of mascara on, and the super good-looking client is about to come through the door. The dog senses your anticipation (hey, we all look forward to the ones that aren't exactly hard on the eyes.) The pooch lets loose with an 'achoo' that could knock you off your stool, if you were one of the lucky few who were able to learn to groom while sitting! Anyhow, now you have little black mascara specks all over your face. Right then, in walks the adonis.

"Hi," you sweetly say as you look up at him, face covered in "worse than slime."

"I think I'll wait out front," he says.

Yeah, those are the good times in grooming. Good thing I met my hubby before I got into this vocation. Little did he know that he was getting a "2-fer" when he amorously nibbled my ear last night...

Chapter 21

Stress

"You ought to take some time off, boss.
You're starting to look like our clients!"

Stress. We all cope with it differently. Some people do yoga. Some do cardiovascular exercise… some of us don't even realize when we are under severe stress. I noticed something was amiss with me the other day. I needed to dry a dog, and before I turned on the force dryer, I reached into a lucite box where I keep grooming bands and foam earplugs. I quickly inserted a pile of rubber bands into my ear. Generally speaking, I prefer to use the earplugs to block the noise. Why I chose to fill my eardrum with latex circles, I don't know. I'm chalking it up to that stress thing.

The usual slow down after Christmas never happened

this year. It's been like the holidays all along. However, we did have one day when there was a terrible ice storm. Almost all the businesses in the area closed, and I did the same. It would do me good to stay home and relax. Wanting to do something different that would help me achieve my goal of de-stressing, I decided to bake cookies. My husband was home that day also. Seeing that he was bored to tears already (8:37 a.m.), I enlisted his help.

"Wanna bake cookies?" I asked happily.

"Do what?" was his reply.

"Cookies… Bake 'em," I said. I also gave him my *look*.

"Sure I do," he wisely replied.

"It'll be our togetherness time," I informed him. I got out the recipes and gave him the one on top. "Read to me, darling," I instructed.

"Four cups of whole-wheat flour…one-half cup molasses…"

"Wait, we don't have any molasses!" I pouted.

"You know how you find some?" he piped up.

"Where?" I asked.

"Go out in the back yard and look down a hole in the ground. You'll find some there," he said grinning.

Every now and then he really is clever. At any rate this wouldn't help with my baking dilemma. A quick trip to the mini market through the frozen tundra solved my problem. However, molasses, usually at about $1.89 in this country was $4.39 in the quickie store. Didn't matter… this was going to be therapy.

Arriving home, I found my hubby had gone back to bed. I knew how to fix that without much hassle. I opened the bedroom door and let three standard poodles jump onto the bed where Prince Charming lay. He was fully awake now.

"Let's do cookies… let's do cookies… don't wanna do cookies!" he mimicked me (badly, I might add).

"Sit!" I instructed, pointing at the kitchen table. Obediently he sat, but I could swear I heard him saying something unfavorable. "Read again," I ordered.

"One-half cup molasses…did I tell you how to find…"

"Yes," I cut him off. "That one's old now. Just read," I

said, impatiently.

"One tablespoon baking soda, one tablespoon ginger, one tablespoon cinnamon," he was saying.

"Gee that sounds like a lot of tablespoons," I commented.

"I'm just reading what it says," Don said, defensively. I pondered the ingredients and starting mixing them together. Instinctively, I stopped.

"Let me see the recipe?" I asked.

You know husbands certainly have their place in marriage. In our case, that place is *not* a kitchen. Just as I suspected, I should have been using teaspoons, not tablespoons.

"Ugh," I grunted. "A big 'T' means tablespoon. These are little 't's'…that means teaspoon," I showed him.

"Big, little, how much difference could it make?" he said defensively. "Have we had enough togetherness yet? Can I go watch TV now?" he asked, like a four year old.

"Fine," I said with a heavy sigh. "Go play." Off he went to the living room, leaving me to roll out my dough.

I cut shamrocks and gingerbread men from the mixture. It rolled out so nicely. Baking was another story. The difference a tablespoon of baking soda can make was very apparent when I took a peek into the oven. I had BIG shamrocks that broadened out to look more like turkeys… The gingerbread men were more like Cyclops. They did smell awfully good, though. This whole project took me about five hours. I made more batches of dough (using teaspoons) and had cookies everwhere. Our dogs sat by my side throughout the whole process. They, of course, got the occasional burnt ones. (My sister called…need I say more?)

"You know, if I were to decorate them, I could take them to the shop and sell 'em," I told my hubby.

"Uh huh," was a reply from a man engrossed in *Indiana Jones* or something. Seven hours later… the decorating was finished… so was the individual wrapping of each one in Saran Wrap.

"Just out of curiosity, how much do you think you need to sell each of those for to make a profit?" Don asked.

I whirled around to look at him, my fingers permanently stained with green food coloring. I noticed a mound of flour on the floor, a few feet in front of me. How it got there I don't have the foggiest. The mess was pretty bad in general.

"It doesn't matter how much I sell them for," I said huffily. "This was our bonding time, and it was relaxing for me," I lied. *Give me a snapping crocodile cocker over this baking stuff any given day,* I secretly thought to myself. You couldn't possibly pay me enough to do this again. All the while my husband was bonding with the recliner, not me. *He* was relaxed.

I packed my precious "labors of love" into boxes and prepared them for selling at the shop. I probably needed to sell them for four times what I did to make an actual profit. I know I went into the proverbial hole on that venture.

I did, however, sell them rather quickly. In less than a week I sold thirteen dozen cookies. It probably helped, having my sign on the display. It read: "These cookies were baked with love by myself in my own little oven. They are healthy treats for your pooch. Please feel sorry for me and buy a few. If you do, I'll feel sorry for you and not raise your grooming price this visit. Have a nice day."

Chapter 22

Doctors

"Save yourself a lot of grief and just let them groom you."

There is such a thing as "burn out" in the grooming industry… or so I hear. I have been lucky up to this point, as I have pretty much enjoyed coming to work for the last few years. Let it suffice to say that I have been at it more than ten and less than eighty years.

This profession is indeed hard on your back, arms, legs and mind. To heal each of the offending organs, I visit the Chiropractor, the M.D. (who often suggests I see a psychotherapist) and the "beer guys" next door. In the case of each, they all have a definite purpose in my meager little life. For the next few stories I will go into detail for you exactly how each of them helps me survive the business. It might not be exactly what you think…

In the case of needing the chiropractor…

You know how those people have the double-coated, must have just moved from Alaska, never seen a slicker brush, been tied outside for as long as I've been alive (*Phew*!) kind of dogs? In comes the beast, looking like "Sasquatch," and there go my arms, shoulders and hands.

"I know he'll be good for you," they are saying, as the dog yanks them through the shop, lifting his leg on anything that isn't moving. Clue #1 that you are in trouble.

"He also hasn't bitten anybody for more than four months now," they are also saying. Definitely Clue #2.

This all naturally happens on a day when you are by yourself. Reason to *never* trust people when they say their dog weighs about twenty-five pounds. Always add a "1" to the front of the "25". Trust me. The twenty-five is just the approximate weight of the hair. They forget to figure the rest of the dog's body in the poundage estimate.

At any rate, after raking this type of animal out (not to mention the fight in the bathtub where the dog discovers there are uses for water other than just to drink), you are spent.

Then there comes the HV dryer. You could move along pretty rapidly on this pet, if only he would stop the "my owner should have given me a hefty dose of Immodium before you turned that thing on" syndrome. As you clean up the never ending cycle of poop, you discover where the extra eighteen pounds or so of the dog came from.

Subtracting seven pounds for excess toenail growth, one pound each for ear crud (there *are* two of them, you know!), and one-half pound for teeth that he is now missing that are embedded in your left arm… we are now down to a respectable 95-1/2 pounds of actual weight. All in all, a far cry from their original 25-pound guess. Now add this dog to the other eight that you did that day. This is where the chiropractor comes in.

The beauty of the Chiropractor that I use is that he was a customer of *mine* first. I remember his first day in here well. As he entered the front door, his dog crapped on the Southwestern theme throw rug at the front door. Right in the center of the diamond turquoise pattern. In a strange way it looked like an abstract piece of artwork. Maybe like something that would be worth millions when the dog died. Gave it an interesting "extra".

At any rate, the Doctor picked up the rug and took it outside, while chastising his dog. When he returned, I calmly asked him what he did with the "deposit".

"I put it in the bushes," he replied.

"Ugh, that won't do," I informed him, as I handed him a bag.

"And I should do what with this?" he queried.

"Well, you should put your hand in it, and pick up the poop. Then you are going to take it with you."

"Huh?" he questioned, not sounding very Doctoral.

"The dog is your property, and the poop belongs to him… therefore, it also belongs to you. You gave it to him, he gave it to me, and I am returning it to the source." I informed him. "You don't think I want it smelling up my place do you?" I added.

Obediently, he went to the bushes and picked up the gift. I smiled as I watched him making disgusted faces. He then gingerly placed the bag in his very new-looking van. It was 83 degrees that day. Hotter in a car, of course. (smile)

I groomed the dog and "Doc" came to pick him up at the appointed time. He scheduled an appointment for five weeks later. It just so happened that the next time he came for the grooming I had my new bather here. He brought the dog in and I took him immediately for his bath. The doctor arrived about fifteen minutes early to pick his pooch up. Now bear in mind that he is a very friendly customer (unlike his pet), so I let him come into the grooming room while I finished his dog.

There was Lou (bather), drying a dog. In the course of the conversation, Doc says to Lou…"I'm gonna pick him off this table and carry him out when he's done. Last time I was here he crapped right on the rug at the door!" he told her in amazement. "I'm not giving him the chance to do that again!" he said emphatically. Lou was nodding her head in agreement.

"Man that stunk like crazy the whole way home. I wanted to throw the bag out somewhere along the road, but figured I'd better not," said Doc. "The heat that day almost cooked that stuff in my back seat… disgusting!" Lou looked at him with a totally perplexed look. "Why did you put it in your car?" she asked. "Because Bonnie told me to. She said I had to clean it up," he informed her. Lou looked at me and started cracking up. I just smiled. Doc looked back and forth between the two of us and was perplexed. "What? What is so funny?" he asked, looking at me.

I just shrugged my shoulders, smiling.

"She doesn't make *anybody* take the stuff home with them. We put it in a bag in the dumpster out back," Lou explained, almost bursting.

"Well then why did you make *me* take it home?" he demanded.

"You're a doctor… you need to be humbled now and then," I explained. Lou and I were laughing so hard, I had tears come to my eyes.

A few weeks ago, my hands both started going numb at night when I slept. I knew it was time for a Chiro visit. It works extremely well for me when I have problems. I am just one of those who can't stand to have my neck messed with.

I arrived for my appointment, and Doc did his usual gentle manipulation of my spine.

"Just don't mess with the neck," I reminded him.

"Of course not," he said. "It really makes your skin crawl when those doctors make it crunch, doesn't it?" he said sympathetically.

"Oh, you know it does," I agreed. With that, he laid my head in his hands and my neck sounded like Rice Krispies as he twisted it.

"Let me hit you!" I squealed. "Why did you do that?" I

asked, in disbelief.

"You're a groomer, and you need to be humbled," he said. This somehow had an all too familiar ring to it.

We have come to an agreement. From now on, if his dog poops in my place, I will clean it up. Doc will never again try to crack my neck... However, if he should forget himself and try that again... I have heard a good one — it is to get skunk urine from a sporting goods shop and place some on a rag. You then place this under the body of a car. I've heard glowing reports on this technology!

Chapter 23

Are You Stressed?

"He's a Dalmatian. Can you paint on some more spots?"

As promised, here is the next story in the line of my secrets to surviving the grooming profession. (I'm sure you have been anxiously awaiting this!)

This story pertains as to why I need visits to my M.D. This is the one that I told you thinks I should also be seeing a psychotherapist. It's not my fault. It's some of my customers who drive me to this point.

I think it's the people with the "notes" and the prescheduled appointment times that drive me to the brink of insanity. You know this kind. Let's take Crickett, for example:

I have been doing this spherical Maltese for her entire life, which has been about twelve years now. The elderly lady who owns her has a standing appointment until I die for 10:00 a.m. on the third Wednesday of each month (If I expire before the dog, I'm sure the owner will be knocking on my tombstone for just ONE MORE WEDNESDAY…). At any rate, the Mrs. shows up each month at 9:15 a.m. for these appointments. Seeing as how I groom one by one, this can tend to throw a crimp in my style. I have this thing about not making a customer wait, either to pick up, or drop off a dog. Yeah, I know… yell at me next time you see me. It's just my way.

I have tried for eleven of the last twelve years to get her to let me make her appointment for 9:30 a.m. at least. You would think I was trying to kill the Pope!

"I couldn't possibly make it that early," she tells me. "I need time to get out of bed and take Cricky to poo," she says.

"But you always get here so early anyhow, that you'd still be fifteen minutes early," I tell her. It falls on deaf ears, so I have pretty much given up. The real kicker in this whole matter is that when she comes to pick up the dog, I always tell her to come back in one hour. This would be 10:15 a.m. for those of you who are really paying attention to this story. Naturally, she arrives to pick up the dog thirty minutes later at 9:45 a.m. Don't ask me how, but I have adapted to this schedule so that the dog is done in thirty minutes. She gets a #3 all over, so it's not that complicated.

But, it is her instructions that I really enjoy. This lady comes in with her dog each time, yet she hands me a handwritten note that is more like a letter. "Dear Bonnie," it says. "Trim Crickett like you always do. Kind of short, but not too short, not down to the skin, but enough so that she isn't too hot. Sometimes she gets too warm in the house, but we don't want her to catch a cold, either. So, cut her hair, just don't cut too much off. But cut enough so that she won't tangle up. You know, I can't believe what it costs to have her hair cut every month! It's more than my own hair! Not that Cricky isn't worth it, but I am a Senior Citizen, you know. Also, give her a bath. I think she is sort of dirty. She might need one… You know, it has been one month since she saw you. I think you should do that thing to her hiney that you do, also. I don't know if it needs poked or whatever you do to it, but do it anyhow, seeing as I am paying for the works. Clean her ears with some cotton, if you would. I use baby oil in them every day. I pour a few drops in to keep them soft inside, so her hair may be a little greasy on her ears. Please trim her fingernails, too. They seem to grow so fast! Can you believe in one month they are sharp again? It doesn't cost any extra for that, does it? Well, I think that is it. Take good care of my baby! – Henrietta"

This is pretty much what my note entails each month. Remember that she brings the dog in herself, so, of course, she repeats every instruction that she already has in her letter. For over a decade now, I have managed to smile when she comes in and when she leaves. I especially like the part when she returns, asking, "Crickett, was the bad groomer lady mean to you?"

Of course you know what I would *like* to tell her…

There is also another lady who brings in an extremely fat beagle mix. The dog is as square as our old coffee table and weighs more than that piece of furniture did. Just hoisting him off the floor is enough to give you a double hernia. His owner also has this thing for certain time appointments. The dog's name is Brutus, but you'd never know it by talking to the owner. She always just refers to him as "The Dog."

A typical phone conversation goes something like this…

"Hello, this is Ann. I need an appointment for the dog's bath."

"How about 10:00 a.m. on Thursday?" I ask.

"No, Thursday's no good for me," she says.

"O.K., how about Friday or Saturday?" I'll say.

"No, I get my hair done on Friday morning," she

is telling me. (I have no idea what's wrong with the afternoon... It's not like she has that much hair or anything!)

"So, would Saturday work?" I ask again.

"I don't think I'll feel like bringing him in then either," she says. "Monday is good for me," she tells me.

"I'm closed on Mondays," I tell her.

"Since when?" she queries.

"Since about twelve years ago," I sweetly inform her.

"Oh," is her reply.

"How about next Wednesday?" I offer.

"That won't work. I bowl," she says.

How she manages to get a ball down the alley, I haven't the foggiest. She claims her knees are so bad that she can't get the dog from the parking lot into my shop. I always have to go out and pick him up and bring him back out when he's done. We aren't even going to get into her laying on the horn the minute she hits the top of the parking area. I feel like Mickey D's with my pick-up and drop-off service with some of these people. The senior set *do* like their car horns.

"Well, Thursday would be perfect for me," she suddenly replies. "How about then?" she asks, as if it were her idea. I am slow sometimes, but wasn't that my original offer? Ugh.

"Oh, that would work for me, too," I say. Double Ugh.

Thursday arrives and I spy Ann pulling into the parking lot. I race out the door to beat her before she has the chance to lay on that Cadillac horn. I wasn't quick enough!

"Hey, Girlie," she says (She has not remembered my name in the last six or seven years!). "My car needs some windshield stuff in it. I don't know how to do it myself," she says. "Here, you do it for me," she orders, handing me a jug of blue stuff. I know... but I did it anyhow. "By the way," she adds, "You won't charge me any extra dollars for cutting the hair around his collar, will you?"

I love my job... I love my job... I love my job...

So eventually I have to give in and go to the doctor for the annual check up. The last time I went in he asked me if

I were having any undue stress.

"Why? Is my blood pressure up? Do I look stressed? Is my pulse okay?" I knew by the look on his face that I was dying.

"I was just wondering if you felt like grooming my schnauzer," he was saying. "He is a great dog, never gave the other groomer any grief," he said.

"Sure," I told him. We finished our conversation, and I started down the hall.

"By the way," he called after me… "My brother's cocker needs done, too. You might have to tie him up… or down… or something," he remarked.

"Is he that bad?" I asked as I spun around.

"Why do you think I asked you if you were stressed?" he grinned at me. I sighed.

Some days you just need a salt-lick of Prozac, ya know?

Chapter 24

What Dogs Have Taught Me

"Comfy?"

Dogs have taught me many things over my lifetime. For instance, when I was nine, I learned never to camp outside with your cousin in a not so well enclosed tent when both your dog and a skunk are in the vicinity. I really couldn't muster the strength to be angry with the Collie, when he was just showing his affection for me by sliding his head across my body. The end result, however, did get me my first official nickname at grade school the next day.

I learned never to bring home the sixth stray dog, as parents do have a breaking point… It ain't pretty!

I learned that you can set a dog's hair in sponge rollers, if you're careful that the dog doesn't eat sponges. This results in a hefty vet bill that comes dangerously close to that parental breaking point again. The dog survived… and I don't mention the lack of judgment on my part. My dad used to say he never understood how he could raise such a dumb daughter. I have two sisters… I think he was referring to one of them.

As I got older, I learned never to buy an Airedale and have a freewheeling mouse in the house. I'm sorry, but not being a rodent lover, I wanted him (the mouse) dead, but I also was kinda attached to the closet door that used to be *whole*. I came home to a top half, but no bottom. Kind of like a Dutch door it was. We keep it as a memento.

Dogs taught me not to bake pumpkin pies for Thanksgiving and put them on the counter overnight to cool. I recall as if it were yesterday, the whole episode. I came out of the bedroom to find my husband staring at the kitchen counter. "What are you looking at?" I queried.

"Didn't you bake some pies last night?" he asked, as he looked into a pair of empty glass plates. I didn't have to wonder too long what happened to the pies. One look at a miserable Airedale told the story. This also explained the smell coming from the downstairs and reinforced the above lesson of the "walking without socks" thing.

The lesson of hanging onto a Flexi with both hands when a deer jumps out ten feet in front of your 72-pound dog was learned pretty quickly. Those 26-footers are murder on human shoulders. The chiropractor seems to like 'em though. This lesson is reinforced when you have shorts on and your dog zooms out around the back of you. Twenty-plus feet of cord searing across the backs of your knees teaches you a whole new meaning to the term "rope burn." Also does something for the term "slow burn" regarding your temper.

I have learned through dogs that they prefer to drink your husband's club soda from his class when he's not looking immediately *after* drinking from the toilet (the dog, not your husband). I withhold the smooching with hubby for awhile after these episodes. The better half hasn't figured it out yet.

I discovered that dogs are uncontrollably drawn to boxes of *Preparation H* suppositories. I do mean BOXES! There went 48 suppositories… foil, box and all. My mother found no humor in this one, but the dog had "s-m-o-o-t-h sailing," so to speak, for days after that one.

I learned through trial and error, that if you want a freshly groomed dog to "go potty," all you do is put him in a newly cleaned cage. I have found if you need them to do #2, put them into a drying cage with a large grate in the bottom. The heavier the better. Put all #1 candidates into a cage without a rack in it. Works on 90% of the cases.

Dogs taught me that there is no meaning whatsoever to the term "obedience trained," when there actually comes a time that you need it. My dog can do all her scent articles and directed jumping with some of the best. I have never really found a time when she might be in a life and death situation and need to "go fetch" that plastic dumbbell from amongst traffic. She knows how to do a perfect front from 50 feet away when called. However, I've tried that when she is chasing a deer through the yard. Dogs really do laugh, you know…

I discovered with my own dog's assistance, that their hearing is very keen. They can hear you bite into a marshmallow from 86.5 yards away. They can even hear you when you are just THINKING of going to *Mickey D's* without them. However, just try calling them to get in the house when you are already late for work. Good luck!

Dogs taught me that your couch was never really yours to begin with. The closest you ever came to actually claiming ownership of it was when you signed that credit card receipt. The minute it hit the front door, it became "Dog Property." I remember looking at the new living room furniture once. As we were leaving the furniture store after purchasing just a lamp, I pointed out the $3,500.00 set to my better half. "Isn't it BEAUTIFUL?" I exclaimed. "So soft!" I groaned as sunk down into the deep cushion of the leather.

"Yeah, it is... the dogs would *love* it," he remarked. That made me shoot out of my comfortable seat like a spring had left loose and hit me in the rear end. Not another word was spoken as we left the showroom. I still have to use "call ahead seating" to use the couch we have now.

On the subject of furniture, the bed is a story in itself. If you want to use it, you have to literally pull the dead weight of dogs off it by their collars. Not until their bodies hit the floor with that unceremonious "thud," do they wake up. I did receive a note from one of them the other day, asking if I could find it in my heart to put complimentary *Milk Bones* on "their" pillows. I think not. Three Standard Poodles in a double bed, along with my hubby guarantees that I am the one who will wake up with the business end of the dog against my face. Yeah, I know.

Dogs have taught me that your veterinarian becomes your best friend. When I go there, they draw a smiley face on my bill, like waitresses do in the restaurant. "Have a nice day" takes on a whole new meaning when you have to make a withdrawal from your savings account to buy a postage stamp. Especially when you realize you don't have a savings account to begin with!

Above all, dogs have taught me that their love for their humans is unending, especially when you are at your lowest point. That saying is true about when nobody else cares, your dog always loves you. They always seem to know when you really need a dog kiss. Never mind that they have just licked their derriere...

Chapter 25

Taking Things for Granted

"Let's be a little more careful where we point that dryer!"

Part One

There are two things one should never take for granted. One is your spouse. The other is your bather. Take as a prime example, a typical day with my husband functioning as my helper. How this arrangement used to work is beyond me, seeing as how we were ready to kill each other after only four hours. The story begins as follows:

Once upon a time, I had far too many animals to groom

by myself in one day. My bather friend, Lou, was unable to come in at the last minute. You must understand that she functions as the "Doggie Savant" when it comes to my needs and those of the clients. I can be in the middle of grooming an animal and suddenly stop for something. Lo and behold, Lou will hand me whatever I am in need of, as if reading my mind (or what's left of it).

She knows precisely the moment that I need her to hang onto a dog when things are going "not so well." She also knows just as well that when I am totally silent, she should come about as close to me as you would to a skunk with a raised tail.

She learned quickly that since the bathing/drying area is rather close to my finishing table, she should be careful when handling the high velocity dryer. I only choked on hair once, that I can recall, from a misdirected blast, and she understood my displeasure.

She knows that I have to have iced tea in the morning since I'm not a coffee person. I am also fond of breakfast burritos, so she almost hits the door with both each morning.

I drop something, and she is there to pick it up before I have the chance to bend over. My daughter witnessed this one day and made a remark to the effect that Lou treats me better than my own kids. I had no reply except for a wry smile. There was some other comment about my being waited on hand and foot. I make a "guffing" sound.

She knows that I am allowed to tease her for her shortcomings, so to speak (She's only 4'11"!). I have been known on occasion to break into my rousing rendition of the "Munchkin's Song" from the Wizard of Oz. I even have that stiff legged little dance down pat. I know she secretly loves this when she's struggling with a large dog in the tub. You can almost see the steam puffs coming from her ears like the Tin Man.

I try to aid her deficit of height by giving her a step aerobics platform for in front of the tub. No matter that I trip over the dumb thing every time I need to use the wash area. I make concessions for her because she's wonderful at what she does.

At any rate, my husband came in on that fateful day. There was the usual once a month for Diamond, the Samoyed. I will say that my husband scooped up the dog and placed her in the tub. That was where is usefulness began… and unfortunately ended.

I washed the dog's left side and went to turn her to the right. Naturally she was about as cooperative as a cow. I struggled to reverse her direction to no avail. Don watched from about three feet behind me. He used to be so good at this stuff. Finally I had her turned and then came the inevitable.

"Do you need me to help you?" he asked innocently.

"No… It's done," I replied between clenched teeth. I rinsed and started to dry the dog. Again, my other half watched. "Don't bother to assist me or anything," I reassured him.

"O.K.," was his reply.

The time came to force-dry the dog. I should have known that it was going to be a fight, and I don't mean on the dog's part. I had to finish a Schnauzer, and left "My Man" to dry Diamond on his own. He dried her in the tub and then plopped her onto the drying table. I saw the equivalent of enough water to supply a small town for a week leaking from the hair on her legs.

"She's not dry, you know," I advised him gently.

"Huh?" was his less than enthusiastic response.

"Look at the mess all over the floor," I chastised him. "You have to clean it up," I informed. Being the great janitor that he is, he naturally spun about thirteen paper towels from the holder. I wasn't even going to go there about the invention of the mop.

He turned on the dryer again in time for me to see the dog's bowels let loose. Oblivious to this bodily function, Husband proceeded to blow it onto the floor. As he stepped on it, I was yelling over the roar of the airflow that she had made a mess.

Smiling, Don nodded at me, obviously not having a clue as to what was happening. When he realized that I was trying to inform him of the situation, he looked down at the floor, and at the same time, lost his aim on the dryer. I had a mixture of Samoyed and Schnauzer hair blown directly into my face. It clung to my eyelashes like cobwebs. As I held up my hand to shield myself, Don remembered that he was aiming the air at me, and quickly redirected the hose… into the trash can, which was chock full of Samoyed undercoat. It looked like a white Christmas!

"Turn it off!" I was really yelling now. He nodded and went to hang up the hose, neglecting to turn it off first. Like a cobra rising up from the basket, it was.

My hubby then tried to clean up the smears on the floor that he had so thoroughly ground into the tile. Naturally, he was just using water on a paper towel. It didn't look good, referring to the floor…or my mood at that point.

"I think I've had enough help for one day," I informed him. "You can go now."

"Fine," was his terse reply, that meant it was FAR from FINE!

He started to stomp toward the door, and I yelled from the grooming room, "Don't I even get a kiss goodbye?"

"I didn't think you'd want one," he snapped. I tell you that kiss had all the romance of two bricks colliding.

At last I was alone, though. As I got on my hands and knees to scrub poop stains from the floor, I thought about Lou. I called her as I scrubbed. She wasn't home, so I just left her a message… "Did I ever tell you how much I appreciate you?" I spoke into her machine. "We need to talk about a raise…"

Part Two

In my shop I have pictures of many of my customer's dogs. I started this many years ago when I first opened. I would take pictures of finished pets, and the ones that came out pretty decent I would have enlarged to 8″ x 10″. Let it suffice to say that I personally feel that I am a much better groomer than I am a photographer. Out of a roll of twenty-four shots, I could usually manage to average seven or eight usable photographs. Most of my subjects were missing an ear, or were enroute to the front door, which left me with a lovely shot of their derriere. Most had the red-eyed demonic look of a wildebeest. I really wasn't very good.

Little did I know that these photos would cause such a ruckus with the townsfolk. It didn't take very long for customers to start bringing in their own photos, which they naturally expected me to frame and display. They began the problem. My valuable wall space that I could be using for retail display was now being used to hang pictures. I had created monsters among my customers. Everyone was getting jealous of everyone else's pictures, and I had no idea how to curtail the problem without offending anyone.

Then the inevitable happened. Retail customers who either had their dogs groomed elsewhere, or not at all, started bringing in *their* pictures. I honestly have picture postcards from thirteen years ago (and accumulating ever since) that people expected me to display proudly forever. I really needed to draw the line at the "groomed elsewhere" pics. At last count, over a year ago, I had 482 doggy pictures. That, my friends, is a *lot* of display. Needless to say, I had to come up with a plan. So… me, being me… I did!

I contracted with a professional photo company to come in and do portraits. I was a nervous wreck the month before the session. I had appointments far exceeding my expectations. Then I had cancellations for the last minute coming out of the blue. So and so were getting divorced and were fighting over doggy custody. In another case, Mrs. What's Her Name's husband was trying to have her committed. She, in turn, was trying to get dirty pictures on her husband, who was supposedly having an affair, and had to cancel the dog appointment since her money was going to the Private Eye. Mrs. Shaffer's dog dropped dead while making its way through the kitchen to its daily pan of bacon grease. Who knew beagles aren't supposed to weight forty-three pounds? People canceled because of last minute vacations, kids need to go off to college, and one lady needed to get braces on her teeth (At 54, I'm not at all sure they were even her own teeth!). Oh, well…

In the end, I had enough appointments that took the place of some of the canceled ones, so I was in the clear. Trying to get everyone's dog groomed twenty minutes before their scheduled picture appointments was a barrel of fun! Naturally, each person showed up early that day, and like dominoes, they all started to run into each other's appointment times.

It was a lot of work, but we had a good time with each person and the pets. I must say both the owner and I were quite surprised that one cantankerous little Peek-A-Poo wasn't thrown out of the back window of the portrait studio. She's a little firecracker of a pooch. In the fifteen years that they have owned her, they have never been able to pick her up like you would a normal eleven pound dog. She wears a harness, and the only way to safely get her into your arms is by attaching the leash and suspending her in mid air. As she dangles helplessly, you scoop her up from behind. Leave me alone… it works!

At any rate, I made the announcement that the professionally done portraits would be taking place of the myriad of pictures currently on my walls. This, I knew, would be a fitting solution to my dilemma, as these would be classy looking and would free up space for my ever-expanding retail section.

We anxiously awaited the next day to see the finished pictures. Everyone was tickled pink with their poochie mug shots. Each person promised me a photo to hang. What came next was not what I envisioned.

I thought I would get a 5″ x 7″ from each owner. What came first was an 8″ x 10″ of a Samoyed. I bought my own frame. Next was another 8″ x 10″ of a Poodle. I bought my own frame. Then came a 4″ x 6″. Disappointed that the first two people brought in larger pictures, this lady decide to compensate for the difference by buying her own frame that was HUGE. It amounted to a 4″ x 6″ photo in an 18″ x 20″ frame. Yeah, a bit out of balance it was…

Following that was a wallet size in an incredibly large, fuzzy, hot pink frame. Another 8″x 10″ came through the door, accompanied by a free easel that stood three feet high. A few days later someone brought two different poses of a pair of Yorkies that were each in its own frame. I can't begin to describe the difficulty I had making those things hang straight. They stuck out like a bow window off the wall.

Of course, when another Yorkie owner saw that her friend had brought in two different pictures, she had to top it by bringing in THREE. I think THOSE frames cost as much as my house!

I ended up with such a mismatched assortment of colors and kinds of frames that I was decidedly no better off now than I was ten years ago. Although the portraits themselves were of a quality that I couldn't exactly match with my own talents. Ahem…

This all started a whole new feud among owners who saw someone's bigger picture than theirs. I stayed out of it. Amid all this controversy of photographs of pets, however there was one final chapter yet to be written. One day Mrs. Kauffman came in with an album of her own. Handing it to me with a huge smile, she made the following proclamation: "I see how much you love to display pictures. I had an extra set of prints made for you of my granddaughter. I thought you might like to share them with your customers. These are for all of you to enjoy!" I flipped through the album, scanning the pictures. The only canines I saw in any of them were in her granddaughter's mouth. (She should have kept her mouth shut, believe me.) "I'm allowing you to choose your own frame," Mrs. Kauffman was saying. "I didn't want to interfere with your décor," she concluded. She left me to ponder this gift. My head in my hands, I knew I was defenseless. I had now become a photo gallery for mutant grandchildren.

So, if you have any extra picture frames lying around…

Chapter 26

The Incredible Shrinking Office

Construction can be a good thing… That is, if you keep my husband away from it. Far, far away. Fortunately, this is easily accomplished by asking him to actually *do* construction. I found, quite by accident one day, that he is what I lovingly like to refer to as "constructionally challenged." I came to this realization the day that he nailed 6" baseboard to the ceiling to the crack between the wall paneling and the ceiling. He called it trim… I called it sad.

He is a wonderful husband. He can fix a washer, dryer, television, radio of any type, automobile, or furnace. He can take apart an entire actual flying airplane and put it back together without having any "extra" parts when he is finished. You just don't let him near any type of wood tool. It has been so long, I have even forgotten exactly where I hid that circular saw. About the only thing I would trust him to construct would perhaps be a coffin for a cockroach or something just as unimpressive (If he sees that I have written this about him, it could be *my* coffin that he will be analyzing blueprints for). At any rate, I decided to take the plunge and expand my grooming shop to enlarge the retail area. This task was placed in the hands of my landlord and his construction company.

At first, it started out quite innocently. My office was to be converted into another retail section and two more areas added to that. It was on a fateful Saturday some five weeks ago that the project began.

I was informed that Friday evening the whole office was to be cleared out so that they could begin knocking out the wall the next day. Like an obedient tenant, I moved everything out of the room and gave it a new temporary home in the hallway… and bathroom… and drying room… and grooming room. It would be fine, I knew. It wasn't going to take them more than a week, so I could live with this arrangement. Ha ha.

My drying room had gone from the capability of holding eleven dogs in cages to harboring two. That is, as long as one of those could be squeezed into a drawer in the filing cabinet that had now taken up residence in the room. You could find him in the file marked "R" for Ridiculously Close Quarters.

My office desk was now in the hall around the corner from the grooming room. I had trained myself within a few days to come in and throw my purse and canvas carry-all thing with enough accuracy to slide under the desk directly in the strike zone. The office chair was in front of the warehouse door and heaven forbid that I would be sitting in it when one of those guys decided to come through there. On more than one occasion, I was unmercifully thumped in the back of the head by that door when they came through unannounced. Once, the door hit the chair with such force that I was propelled out of it much like one of those suction cup darts shot from a plastic gun. My knee still hurts now and then where I cracked it on the door jamb. Never mind the time I almost had the end of my tongue amputated when I bit down through it after another entrance. I learned to be very aware of letting my guard down when I sat there.

The hallway is "L" shaped, and turning the corner to go down toward the bathroom was another hazardous area. Thankfully, I have lost a few pounds as you had to get to the corner and turn sideways to maneuver down the rest of the hall.

I KNEW there would come a time when the value of country line dancing would come into play. It was a shame I was too uncoordinated to learn it when it was popular. It's okay, though. I invented my own moves. Oh, the things some of my customers got to see me do. I was entertaining to say the least.

The view you had in the bathroom was a story in itself. Sitting on the "throne" you were surrounded by cases of cow parts. Ears, cheeks, tendons… you name it, it was all conveniently close by. Stacked to the ceiling the boxes were. A German Shepherd could have survived for 10 months in that room on pure beef.

Then there was the plastic sheeting. This was taped over the old office opening so that all the drywall dust that the guys were creating wouldn't go all over the retail merchandise that was already on display. Just about the time I would have it sealed off completely, somebody would have to come through it for a bucket or something. I had to dust everyday. One week soon stretched into three, and my patience was waning. I was getting like a rubber band that has been sitting in the sun. My pleasant personality was beginning to crack under the strain.

One of the worst days was when I decided to help the guys out by cleaning up some of the drywall dust that was in huge drifts on the floor in the plastic encased room. I trudged in there with canister sweeper in hand, minus the floor attachment, so that I would have more suction with just the wand as the end. Because it was such a tight area where most of the dust piles were, I left the canister part of the sweeper out in the retail section on the other side of the plastic. I vacuumed for about 15 minutes straight in there, there was that much dust. I hit the foot switch on the sweeper as I exited back through the plastic and looked up. I was like what heaven must be… I walked into a giant cloud. In my defense, no one ever told me that you can't suck that stuff up with an ordinary sweeper… that it somehow passes right through the filter and back out the blow hole in the canister. I cried. I now had four solid hours of cleaning ahead of me to rid the shop of the mess I had deposited on every bottle, every collar, every *everything* in the place. It was like Mount St. Helens had erupted in there. It was bad!

Four weeks into the project, I was seeing that maybe psychiatrists *do* serve a useful purpose in life. That maybe

Valium didn't deserve such a bad rap. That the definition of hemorrhoid could apply to some of the people in the building trade. That maybe my husband wasn't actually dense when it came to construction after all. Maybe he had known something all alone that I failed to realize… He valued our marriage too much to even approach building tasks. It would have been the demise of our relationship if *he* had left those 2x4's leaning on the grooming room door that hit me over the head when I opened it one day. That *both* eyes *can* turn black and blue when you get elbowed by a guy carrying a sawhorse backwards and you crack yourself in the eye with the side of the doorknob. The irony of it was the doorknob wasn't even *on* the door at the time. Don't ask… just believe.

After 38 days of thumping, bumping, pounding, sanding and sawing (not to mention swearing on *somebody's* part… who shall be nameless), the project was completed. I now had what I must say is a beautiful place to spend all those long hours each day. Actually, it was ideal to begin with but has now doubled in size.

For the last two days I have found myself walking in and still throwing my purse "bowling-like fashion" down the hallway to its rightful place under the desk. But alas, the desk is no longer there. The refrigerator is not in the aisle either. Nor are the wiggly, giggly balls that kept falling from their precarious perches and scaring the crap out of us. I'll miss their little laughter as they rolled down the pathway. The cow remains are all tucked away in their rightful displays, waiting to please some little pooch after a hard day's work of chewing up someone's garbage can treasures. Gone are the days of having shampoo bottles to read when you were "concentrating" in the bathroom. Sigh.

Today, however, I heard a snappy little tune on a country radio station as I was mopping the floor. I just couldn't help myself… I did my own little version of the "Electric Slide" down the hall. Never mind that I may have done some permanent damage to my elbow when I slid into the steps going up into the bathroom… Ahhh, the good old days…

Chapter 27

Where's the Poop?

"The $50 is for grooming your dog,
the $365 is for the grooming equipment your dog ate!"

You know how some days just seem to drag on forever when you're busy… and then there are the "When did all the other groomers die?" days. Those that I affectionately refer to as "Bag" days. These are the days when every animal that walks through the front door decides that your place is like that giant fire hydrant in the sky. Take last Tuesday for instance. That was right before Easter. Mrs. Cramer walked in and Muffy promptly pooped on the door. Not on the floor in front of the door... *on* the door. This dog has this incredible talent for backing right up against a wall, fence, or in this case, door and letting it all out. You should have seen her the day I witnessed her backing up on some guy's Corvette. She parked her rear end right in the guy's mag wheels and let loose. Normally, I frown upon such behavior, but he was parked in my allotted spaces and went into the restaurant next door. What-ever.

At any rate, I yelled for Lou. "Delivery for you, Lou," I yelled into the back room.

"Delivery for me?" she asked with a puzzled look. I pointed to the door. Giving me an evil smile, she reached for a disposal bag. I reached for the dog. As I pulled Muffy along to the grooming room, I noticed a yellow trail following her.

"Here are a couple more paper towels," I offered.

"Gee, you're all heart," Lou commented.

"I know," was my reply.

Our method here for disposing of our client "gifts" is to bag them and put them into a landscape timber arrangement outside the building. At the end of the day, we put each of these into a bigger bag and cart it off to the dumpster. As far as I can recall, the record was a nine-bag day. That was at Christmas about two years ago. What can I say? I guess we were really blessed that year.

All the old customers know what the bags mean. They'll come in and make comments like, "You must be really busy today. I see you have quite a few 'packages' outside." I'll never forget the time Mrs. Shumaker got her initiation. Outside were several "deposits," and when she was leaving, she picked them all up and brought them back inside. Now to really appreciate the situation, you must first picture this seventy-eight year old woman in a full length mink coat carrying in three bags. She placed them on the counter and said, "I found these outside the building. Do they belong to you?"

"Well, not directly," I told her.

"Oh?" was her quizzical replay. "What are they?" she inquired, picking up one of the bags while sort of squeezing on it.

"Dog poop," I stated, in the unnerved way that I do.

"Ughhghgh!" she yelled, while dropping the bag onto the floor. "I wouldn't have picked them up if I had known!" she exclaimed.

"Naturally," I said, grinning.

Anyhow, back to the gist of the story. I groomed Muffy, and then Rusty and Sparkle came in. Lou came out to take them from Mrs. Shaver, and I casually mentioned something about Rusty liking to poop in your pocket when you picked him up.

"What?" Lou was saying as she turned the corner down the hall.

"I said he sometimes likes to poop in your pocket if he gets too nervous." She stopped and gave me a "quit trying to put one over on me" kind of look. About forty-five seconds later (give or take a millisecond or two) I heard the exclamation of the short person I know and love so dearly.

"I told you so," I said as I strode past the doorway. I tossed a bag to her on my way to the office.

Mrs. King arrived with Jacque shortly after 11:00 a.m. I placed him in the tub and fastened him to the wall. I went back to my table to finish Sparkle, and Lou walked over to begin bathing Jacque. I glanced over her way in time to see her leaning on the side of the tub while hanging her head in a defeated manner.

"What's wrong?" I queried. I received no reply from her. Just a heavy sigh as she was passing me with a white package in her right hand. I heard the front door bell ring as her little footsteps sounded mighty heavy on the tile floor.

The day went pretty smoothly from then on until about 2:30. I didn't have many dogs left to groom, and Lou was finished with all her "batherly" duties. She opened the door to the cage room, and I'm not sure if the smell hit me first, or if I heard her "less than Sunday school" remarks. Four dogs… four dirty cages… sixteen feet to re-wash. One big bag to add to the landscape timber pile. I have nothing to tell you about our conversation that occurred when she was cleaning up the mess. Suffice it to say, it wasn't repeatable.

We were running low on large trash bags, I noticed, so we used an empty box that had once contained dog toys. A colorful box it was, and we "loaded" our "loads" (Ha ha!) in it to take to the dumpster.

"Just go home," I instructed Lou. "I'll take it down when I leave," I offered. Receiving no argument from her on that, she left.

My hubby stopped in before he went home to take care of some errands for me before the end of the day. I was trying to clean up the shop and myself before I quit and gave him a quick smooch good-bye.

Later that evening, as we sat watching TV, Don suddenly recalled what he had been trying to remember over dinner. "Oh, you know those boxes I took to UPS this afternoon for you?" he questioned.

"Yeah ..." was my disinterested reply.

"You forgot to put a label on one of them," he was saying. I quickly ran through my mind the boxes that were to go that day.

"No ... they all had addresses," I told him.

"No," he insisted. "There was one that had dog toys in it at one time. You forgot to put any label on it." Yeah, it suddenly dawned on me which box was "homeless."

"Oh, _______! What did you do with it?" I asked in a panic.

"I just left it at the drop off and told Cindy you would call her tomorrow with the address. No biggie," Hubby was saying. "What's the big stink?" he queried.

If a person could ever die from laughter, now was the time ...

Chapter 28

The Hospital

"Pets can be very useful in the healing process!"

It was bound to happen at some point. You know… we all wind up in the hospital for something or other. The last time I was in was when I was thrown from a horse while he was galloping across an area littered with rocks that were five and six feet across. Yeah, he dumped me about as unceremoniously as you could get right onto one of those rocks head first. I don't remember that incident at all, but was told by a friend I was riding with that I landed with all the grace of a duck shot out of the sky. They don't glide elegantly through the air when they are plunging to the ground. Apparently, I didn't either. Anyhow…

My hubby had to go to the hospital for what turned out to be kidney stone removal. The technical name for the procedure is a cystoscopy. I can never recall that term, so I dub it a pe***oscopy. At any rate, I took him in for this at 5:30 a.m. Needless to say, he wasn't happy that he was having to have this done at all. Also, he was less than thrilled about the time we had to be there and the fact that he wasn't allowed food or drink since the night before. I tried to be my compassionate best as his sole support for this endeavor. On the way in, I took his hand in mine. "Do you mind if we stop at the drive-thru at McDonald's so I can get a burrito and a coffee?" I asked softly. Now, I don't even really drink coffee… It just seemed like the right thing to say. I felt it paid him back for all the times I was starving myself on cabbage diets and the like, while he ate scampi and cheesecakes in front of me. He is a coffeeholic. He wasn't smiling.

No, I didn't go there. It was all in the name of harassment. Anyhow, we arrived at the hospital, and I really started doting on him from the moment his feet hit the parking lot. I opened his door for him as he went to get out of the car.

"I can open my own door," he said, waving me away. I knew he was nervous. I took it in stride. As we headed for the door to the outpatient department, I placed his arm in mine to help him onto the curb.

"I'm not an invalid or anything. I can make it up this four inch step all by myself," he said testily.

"No, nothing's broken yet," I was thinking silently. A few more snippy remarks out of him, and I'd put in my own request for the Urologist's duties on him!

We entered the waiting area, and who was working as the volunteer for the day in that department but my best doggy client, Mrs. Shumaker.

"Oh, I've been worried that you overslept," Jewel said. I got you a room with a new recliner. I mean they are *brand new*. Some are a beautiful blue print and others are solid blue. They're soooo comfy," she was going on.

"Huh?" Don was saying. "Since when do patients get recliners instead of beds?" he queried.

"Oh, not for you, Don," Jewel said. "I meant for Bonnie. Wait until I tell everyone you're here," she said. She was so happy.

Don was smiling. "Come now, I'm not that important," he said grinning.

"I meant that Bonnie is here," she sniffed at him. "Everyone!" she announced as she opened the door to the nurses' station. "My dog groomer is here! Missy's beautician has arrived!"

I felt like royalty. Don glanced at me and gave his best snooty look. You know, one of those with the pursed lips kind of thing. "Well," he huffed. "Aren't you of importance?"

"Oh... just so-so," I said, glancing at the magazine assortment.

Jewel reappeared and signed Don in. "Come back with me, and they'll get you undressed," she told him.

"Oh, r-e-a-l-l-y?" he chuckled, glancing my way. "Good looking nurses, I hope." He put his hands in his pockets.

"Yes, they're good looking," she said. "But you have the male nurses today." He looked alarmed.

"Can I come too?" I asked.

"Don't even ..." my hubby was saying as he was pulled through the double doors. I settled into my chair in the waiting room until they called me in to wait with him in his room. About ten minutes passed, and Jewel came through the lobby with a good looking guy in tow.

"This is Doctor Shaulis," she informed me. I reached out to shake his hand, and Jewel immediately took it.

"This," she proclaimed, "is Missy's hairdresser."

"We have heard all about you," Dr. Shaulis was saying. "You groom that sissy dog of Jewel's?"

"That would indeed be me," I grinned. Dr. Shaulis explained the intricacies of Don's pe***oscopy to me, and I was instructed to follow him back to the outpatient rooms. Finding my hubby all tucked into his bed in his pretty little hospital "dress," I headed for his bedside.

"Are you all right?" I asked, figuring he was getting kind of nervous at this point. I leaned over to give him a loving peck on the forehead.

"Don't fuss. I'm perfectly fine," he quipped. If I would have had access to a mallet, I would have konked him on the noggin at that point… "Don't fuss"… ugh!

Nurses, both male and female came in and out. One gave an IV. Another made him sign consent forms. The anesthesiologist came in to explain what type of sedation they would give Don. As soon as he left, my hubby demonstrated all the territorial instincts of a terrier.

"Did you notice that guy was talking to you, not me? He wasn't interested in telling me anything. He explained it all like you were having the operation. He totally ignored me," Don complained.

"Oh, he did not! You just don't respond when people talk to you sometimes. You act like you're comatose or something," I explained.

"Well, you're more important today anyhow. After all, you're the Dog Groomer," he whined. Where was the nurse in charge of giving enemas, I wondered? I was willing to pay extra at this point!

Jewel appeared in the doorway of the room with some more nurses and a proctologist. The proctologist spoke up. "So, we hear you are Missy's …"

"Yeah, she's the dog's hairdresser," my husband shot across the room before the doctor could finish his sentence. Oh, a proctologist could give a mighty fine enema, I was betting.

"You have to quit telling everyone that, Jewel," I said, as I gave her a mini hug. "Don's getting jealous," I smiled at him.

"What's that?" he asked from his bed.

"Nothing, Sweetie," I said. I sat quietly in my little corner until they came to wheel my loving hubby away. I worriedly watched TV and paced until an hour passed and the nurses were wheeling Don's bed back down the hall.

"He did great. He had a kidney stone, and Doctor will be in to talk to you shortly about what he did for it," one nurse explained.

Don was so out of it. He slept and awakened, then slept some more. Finally, he came to enough to know something wasn't quite the same as when he had come into the hospital that morning.

Just then Dr. Shaulis entered the room, along with a nurse. "Don had a rather large stone that I crushed," he explained. "We need to make sure that he passes the rest of the stone, so he has a catheter in for a few days."

"I have what in where?" the not-so-patient patient bellowed from his prone position. He complained for five minutes about the thing while the doctor explained what we needed to do in relation to the "thing" over the next day or so.

Needless to say, Don was totally embarrassed by this whole process. However, my sweetest revenge was yet to come for the way he treated me while I was babying him that morning.

"Let me explain to you what you need to do here," the doctor was saying to me. He lifted the sheet and there we were. The doctor, the nurse, the charge nurse and I were all peering down at "it." I glanced up at Don. He face was never that red in eighteen years of our marriage. Doctor Shaulis was pointing to the tube from the catheter, and the anatomical part of my husband that it was connected to was in full view of the four of us.

Suddenly the charge nurse pointed a finger at me. "Oh, my gosh, are you the same Bonnie Wonders that grooms Jewel's dog?" she asked in surprise.

"Yes, she is," Dr. Shaulis was nodding to her.

"She sent all of us a Christmas picture of Missy last year. You do such nice work," the nurse was saying. "You know, I have a poodle mix, and I'd love to see what you could do with her. How much does it cost to get her groomed like Missy?" she was asking. All the while, the doctor was holding up the sheet on my poor husband's "Ambrose," as Jewel calls it.

You had to picture it. Four of us talking dogs and my beet-red husband's "part" lying there as we absently stared at it. "Can I have my sheet back?" Don suddenly broke into our conversation.

"Oh, sure," one of the nurses said. "Sorry." She laid the sheet to rest.

They discharged Don shortly after that and as we headed down the hall, a nurse came trotting up behind us.

"Mrs. Wonders?" she asked as she caught up to us.

"Yes, she's Missy's dog groomer," my husband said. "Sure, she'll be happy to cut your dog's hair," he offered.

"Well, that's all real nice," she said, "but I don't have a dog. I just wanted to give you your book. You left it in the room. It's nice that you're so supportive of your wife, though," she said admiringly.

"Isn't it?" I said, smiling up at my husband.

"You can lock me in the car now," Don said. "The trunk will be just fine."

Chapter 29

Skunked Again!

"I'm tired of having to beg.
Now take me to my groomer!"

Many of my customers become close friends, as I'm sure yours do. I get invited to baby showers, weddings and birthday parties. I get phone calls in the middle of the night with questions that are of the veterinary nature. I actually had one lady call me late one night, asking one of the most bizarre questions I ever had to field. When she had to slam on her car brakes, her male dog hit the dashboard, and she inquired if he could have broken his "part!" She said it didn't look as "big" to her as it had the day before. Sigh... Some people have far too much time on their hands, if you ask me.

I've driven to work in the middle of the night to de-skunk a dog that got sprayed the night before a funeral. The people who owned the dog also owned the funeral home. I had to do it. Can you imagine going in to view a body that smells like skunk? It would have killed a lot of future business for them, I would guess. Ohhh, that was a bad pun…

At any rate, skunks seem to be pretty prevalent in this area. Last week I received a phone call from a customer who brings the dog in every Friday for a bath. I got to work at 7:00 a.m., and there was an urgent message on the machine from Mike. "Cody got sprayed by a skunk last night," he was saying. "We've put him in the barn for now. What do you want me to do with him?" he was asking. I called him back to tell him to bring the dog in right away, and I could bathe him before my other appointments started showing up. He was so relieved, and within ten minutes, Mike appeared at the shop. He came in alone. "The dog is in the bed of the truck," he was saying. "Are you ready for him?" he asked.

"Go ahead. Bring him in and deposit him into the tub," I told Mike. He whipped a pair of Playtex gloves from his back pocket and headed outside.

In he carried poor little Cody (a mini poodle) at arm's length. I immediately put full strength de-skunker on the usual places they get sprayed. He was definitely ripe. I let him sit for ten minutes and then rinsed. I re-bathed him two times and was satisfied with the results.

At 8:55 a.m. I called over to the beer distributor next door. "Can you bring me your can of Lysol?" I asked Steve.

"Oh, my gosh!" he exclaimed. "Can you smell it in your place, too?" he was asking.

"Huh?" I said, puzzled.

"I went into the warehouse with Rich and a skunk must have gotten in there last night," he said "The whole place smells like skunk!" he exclaimed.

"Ohhhh," I said, wondering what to say next.

At that moment it occurred to me that if the warehouse stunk so badly that the "Hair Girls," as we refer to them, who own the beauty shop next door to me had probably noticed it, too. This was better than an average possibility, seeing as how I had the exhaust fan on, which is directly routed into the warehouse. Also, the air conditioner was running and it is exhausted between our outside walls, also into the warehouse.

I quickly ran out to the font room and looked outside in the direction of the beauty shop. I saw several of their clients standing outside the shop, waving their hands in front of their faces. Ohhh, I could be in trouble, I thought. My immediate plan was to deny any wrong doing and act totally innocent of any accusations.

Within a few minutes my phone rang, and it was from one of the tenants upstairs. "You wouldn't happen to know anything about the smell that seems to be emanating from the building, would you?" the guy was asking me.

"Uhhh, I think someone mentioned something about a skunk passing through the warehouse last night," I casually told him.

Gee... Now when some guy buys beer from the distributor here, I guess it gives a whole new meaning to the term "getting skunked" on beer. Ha ha!

Chapter 30

Iced Tea

6:50 a.m. – I stop at Mickey D's for my usual iced tea (super size, no less), as my trusty little helper won't be in until 9:00 a.m. Yeah, I'm too good to her. I know full well, however, that I won't last until she arrives if I have to do without my daily drink.

I get to the shop at 7:01 a.m., and my first dog, scheduled for 7:30, is already waiting in the parking lot. Out pops Muffy's owner with a large container from where else but McDonald's.

"Muff knows how much you love your tea, so she brought you this," the dog's owner, Pat, was saying. Trying to hide the huge drink I already had in my hand, I slipped it into the canvas tote that I carry each day. Wouldn't it just figure that when this woman is normally in such a huge rush to get to work, she would pick this day to go in late! I thanked her profusely for the drink as I tried desperately to keep the canvas bag completely still so I wouldn't knock over the cup inside. I wasn't too successful. I stood there talking to Pat while keeping the bag in front of me, sandwiched between my purse and my stomach.

Soon I began to feel as if I should have tucked a Depends into my drawers. I could feel tea trickling down my leg and into my left sock.

"I really need to go, Pat," I said, hobbling to the front door of the shop.

"I see," she said in an abnormal tone. The

embarrassment of it all! This I did in the name of appreciation for my customer's thoughtfulness. Oh, well…

I got inside and fished the cup out of the tote bag. It amazingly was still almost half full. At a buck sixty-two, I was not about to waste the rest. I have one of those little "cubie" kinds of fridges in the office. You know the kind. They hold about four sandwiches (if you stack them) and a six pack of soda or whatever else might be sold in six pack form (ha ha), an apple and three ice cubes. At that point, one of those things is maxed out on space.

At any rate, I put Pat's gift inside "cubie" and went to work. At 7:55, my next appointment arrived.

"Here," Lindy said, as I came around the corner. "A peace offering from the last time when Rex drank yours when you weren't looking," she said. Lindy handed me a familiar looking plastic cup of… you guessed it.

"Oh, how sweet," I gushed. "You know I really do love my tea," I said, smiling broadly. "Exactly how was it that Rex was able to get into my drink, anyhow?" I asked, trying to envision this one.

"Oh, you know, '… happens,'" she said as she scooted out the door, leaving me with a Cocker Spaniel looking up at me as he hiked his leg onto the side of the front counter. I sighed.

I added my latest gift to Pat's and went to work. I was in the midst of finishing my "Tote bag tea" when Lou walked in.

"Here's your burrito and iced tea," she said, plopping them both onto the spare grooming table. "You would be so proud of me" she was saying. "I forgot the tea, of all things, and had to go around the drive-up again just to get it. I knew you'd be ticked off if you had to go without. I rushed like crazy so I wouldn't be late. Did I do good?" she was asking like a five year old. Geez, I didn't have the heart to tell her that I had two others waiting in the fridge.

"You were outstanding," I told her. I ditched the now empty cup from number one into the trash. I smiled as I squeezed lemon into my beverage.

Within five minutes of Lou's arrival came the next client. My bladder started swelling at the sight of what came through the door, along with a Maltese. I mustered a big smile of appreciation.

"Mazie and I knew you'd be thirsty already. It's getting pretty warm out there, so we stopped for your morning tea," Mr. Bowers said proudly. This guy is good. He had the lemon in a separate cup, six packets of Equal, six sugars, six Sweet 'N Lows, an extra cup of ice and one stirrer to boot. All this in a carry all container. "I couldn't remember what you use to sweeten it so I got some of each," he gave me a big grin.

Lou came out right about then, and it occurred to me that I had never seen human eyebrows go quite that far up on a face. Anyhow, I gave Mr. Bowers a quick hug for being so sweet and acted as though I was dying of thirst right then and hurriedly dumped three of the Equals into the tea. I took a huge gulp as I downed some of the cold caffeine. Mr. Bowers left and I ran back to the bathroom. "I'll be right back," I told Lou.

Heaving a big sigh, I took my newest acquisition to the fridge. I now had three huge drinks waiting in there for me, plus the one in the grooming room that Lou had run around like the proverbial headless chicken for. I wasn't about to let her know about the others in hiding.

I was almost finished with dog number three (and tea number two) when Cathy Meyers came in ricocheting off the front door. As I looked up through the one way glass in the grooming room, I saw her trying to regain her balance while handling an all-too-familiar sight. There in her little hands, in addition to her dog's leash to which there was attached a Poodle was a genuine, certified honest to goodness grey carton containing not one, but *two* supersized you-know-whats.

"One for you and one for Lou," Cathy was saying. I was going to need a catheter attached to me soon!

"Lou doesn't ever drink tea," I thought to myself. Once again I found myself thanking yet another thoughtful client. Why these people are so good to me often baffles me. They are constantly feeding me. I get everything from hot meals brought in during the winter to subs in the summer. I get homemade jelly and pickles, cheesecakes, cookies of every imaginable kind, candy and of course, tea. I think the tea thing got its start from when customers tell me where they're going while I do their pets. They always ask if I want anything, and I usually request a drink. It's just that it has never happened that I get so many all at the same time. It's sometimes hard to be humble when you're this popular!

I was happily grooming away when Lou went out front and noticed that I had forgotten to put the latest acquisition away. "You know you'll have to drink mine, too," she was saying as she headed back to the office.

"What are you doing?" I asked as I suddenly realized what was going to happen when she opened the fridge. I heard the office door shut a little harder than was necessary and witnessed the demise of several objects fly past me into the tub.

"And that would have been???" I mumbled.

"Three ice cubes that lost their happy home..." she retorted.

Chapter 31

Holiday Spirit

I love the holidays. I love the manger scenes, the religious cards, the whole aspect of the true meaning of Christmas. I also love the lights, the trees and the general feeling of happiness at this time of year.

I try to help spread the happiness. Take the other day, for instance. There I was, in a tremendous burst of holiday spirit. I went shopping for lights to decorate the front of my shop. I bought swag lights (two sizes), icicle lights, plain clear lights, colored string lights and tubular lights. In total, I had one hundred twenty-three feet of lights. I should tell you now that my shop's bow window is a total of four feet long. Yeah, a bit of overkill, I guess. I took out the swag lights. Have you ever tried to figure out how to untangle those things? I spent twenty-three minutes trying to separate them, only to discover they were twelve inches too short. The next set was twelve feet in length. Once I had *them* figured out, I learned they were too long. In the end, I decided to use the multi-colored strand. It would be perfect... once I figured out how to use all twenty-seven feet on a four feet wide window. Being the woman that I am, I designed the perfect display of lights that would criss-cross the window at all the right places and use each light to the very end. It fit perfectly. It took me forty-two minutes. It was hard!

I was so excited. It really was a work of art that I knew would look classier than just lights going squarely around a window frame. I called Steve from next door.

"I'm gonna light my window," I said excitedly. "Come watch and tell me how good they look," I invited him.

"Okay. I'll be in the parking lot!" he said with glee. He tries to appease me as per the landlord's instructions. I pay my rent on time, so they like me here. Out he came and stood in the freezing cold.

There I was fumbling with the extension cord, trying to untangle it as my fingers wouldn't work quite right in my haste. I looked out to see him tapping his foot impatiently as he stood with no coat on. O.K! I plugged it in... You know what happened next. My smile turned to a grimace. Steve shook his head and ran into his office. I pushed on every bulb, shook every wire and monkeyed with the extension cord. Nothing. I was so disgusted. At least Chevy Chase got paid handsomely when it happened to him in *Christmas Vacation*! I got squat.

I unceremoniously ripped the lights down from their place of honor in the window. I plugged them in again after I had them down, just to see if they ironically would light after all. Nothing. Figuring I should maybe groom a dog or two, I started to work.

In walked my bather. "What happened to the big light display? I thought you went to get some yesterday," she queried.

"They don't work," I snapped. She disappeared into

the office and returned, draped in strands of multi-colored lights. As is with the law of averages or Murphy's Law or *something* like that, they naturally lit immediately for her.

"Just a suggestion," she was saying, "when you put them up, leave them lit so if they go out, you kinda know where the problem is." She thinks she's this master electrician, or something, I guess. To appease her, I did as she instructed. Never mind that I forgot how I originally put the things up with my design. This again took me another thirty-eight minutes to figure it out. I was seriously falling behind in my grooming duties, but my window got finished and looked professional. I was really in the holiday mood now!

We worked on dogs, and I remembered that I had purchased two new Christmas CD's when I was on my light buying spree. I ran into the office and ripped the cellophane off the discs. I loaded them into the player and the carols began. I cranked up the music and opened my back door to the warehouse for all the beer guys to enjoy. You have to understand that when I open that door, it is every man's dream of paradise in there. There is usually nothing but beer as far as the eye can see! Cases of beer stacked so high I can often only see the ceiling from my doorway. This particular day there were three guys loading beer onto delivery trucks.

"Ho ho ho! How'd ya guys like my music?" I yelled cheerfully. One guy totally ignored me another one was shaking his head while loading a dolly full of cases, and I swear that airborne can of Coors Light was aimed at me from the third. I sensed they were having no appreciation for me at that very moment.

All dogs, of course, had to have holiday bows on. Whether you like bows or not, the rule here is that your pooch can't leave without one. And to that guy who said his "dog ain't looking like no elf dog at Christmas," I say, "Be careful when you bite into that holiday chocolate. You never know if some Ex-Lax might have found its way into the batch. Fa la la la la..."

The amount of new customers we pick up over the holidays is gratifying. The new ones usually have the best stories, though. In walked one today, for instance. "Be careful Harriet doesn't poop on you," the lady was telling me. "She ate a box of sugar cookies, a pack of gum and some sausage that my husband left on the counter. Oh, dear, and part of a box of Immodium!"

I shook my head in disbelief. "She ate all of this at once?" I said in disbelief.

"Within the last hour or so," she sighed. I must say the dog looked pretty rotund. I did the grooming without incident. My guess is that the Immodium kept her from exploding.

The first official gift of Christmas came for me just yesterday. In walked Mrs. Fieg with her pug, Betsy, to be groomed. In tow were her six-year-old twins. They came bearing a Christmas themed plate on which sat one Hershey Kiss cookie and one partially eaten Hershey Kiss.

"And this would be..." My question trailed off into the distance.

"What's left of your gift from Betsy," Mrs. Fieg was saying. The twins were giggling. Betsy winked...

Happy Holidays to you all. Happiness at this time of year... I try to help spread the happiness!

Chapter 32

Flirts

"I've never dated a dog groomer before."

Grooming is a very demanding profession. There are so many hats the average groomer must wear, including those that would fall under the heading of Marriage Counselor, Dating Service Coordinator and Psychiatrist. You have to listen to who is cheating on whom; who might be cheating on whom, and who should be cheating on whom. Not that it matters at all to you, mainly because you don't even know any of the parties involved. I find myself nodding in agreement with whomever it is that is paying the grooming bill. Hey, money talks.

There are, however, times when female groomers, like in any other profession, get hit on. Sometimes it lifts your spirits to know you are still desirable even though you have more rings around your eyes than a Sequoia. Sometimes, however, it makes you feel like the green stuff that grows in the back of your fridge. OK… in the back of *my* fridge.

There was the guy whom we shall call "Mike" (name not changed to protect anybody, anyhow) who barged in one day to tell me he and his wife were "splitting the sheets." I wasn't touching that one, as I figured it to be vulgar in one way or another. I didn't feel like guessing precisely what it meant. Turned out that it was his way of saying they were getting a divorce.

At any rate, this rather large, burly, bowlegged and pigeon toed man started popping in to see me on a rather frequent basis. Believe me, I ain't no prize, but gimme a break. He would say, "She said I was a good for nothin'. Do you think that's true?" Now what could I possibly say other than smile and offer something like, "Of course not!"

He would bring his dog in and stand around watching me bathe her and say something really original like, "If I climb into that tub, would you soap me up, too?" How many times have you girls heard that one?

The final straw came when I saw him out of the corner of my eye in the grocery store one day. There I was… innocently looking for cream of rice cereal for the latest fad diet (never mind) and although I tried to slink into the opposite direction from him, I was spotted.

"Hey," he said, "are you out spending all that money of yours?"

"Uh, yeah. A girl's gotta eat, you know," I said, matter of factly.

Those ugly duck-like feet waddled over next to me in no time flat. "Hey, you otta try the variety pack of these instant oatmeals. They're real good," he informed me.

"Thanks. I'll do that," I said, tossing a box into my cart. An unwanted box of cereal was a small price to pay to get me out of there.

"Gee, you sure look different when you're not at work," he was saying. "R-e-a-l good," he said, drawing out the real part. Oh, sure. In a world full of eligible men I would get one that looked like a penguin.

"Well, thanks, but I gotta run," I told him. I looked like a white Flo Jo running down the aisle (Well, I would have looked like her if I had a good body, hair and nails that didn't look like I had been scratching my way out of a beaver dam).

I persevered, however. I have learned to be on the phone whenever he comes around to chat. It seems to be working…

I will always less than fondly recall the guy who came in one day and asked me some innocent enough grooming questions. I patiently answered all of them and suddenly he complemented me on my colorful grooming smock.

"Thanks," I said non-commitally.

"Is that a uniform or is that more like a shirt?" he was asking.

"It's a smock," I said, shrugging my shoulders.

"But, so you wear anything under it, or not?" he queried. This was getting kinda freaky, and I thought of whom to turn to if I needed help, should this guy really be a nut case.

"Yeah, right," my subconscious told me. I'm the one they call when they get abnormal being in their place. Not that Steve isn't a real macho kind of guy. Actually, he can get a lot accomplished when he's crouching in fear under his office desk. If Pennsylvania ever has an earthquake, his life would be spared under that monstrosity. I still recall the day he had to lift a keg of beer into the back of a delivery van. Just who do you think he called to help him lift it.

"But it's so heavy," he whined.

This really makes me recall the times that I've been in need. Several times I have needed some extra muscle when I'm trying to lift a 140-pound wildebeest thing into the tub. I call over there and ask for a little help, and he send poor little Cliff to help. I do Pomeranians that outweigh that guy.

"I'll be back for your help with something," he said as he turned to leave. I breathed a sigh of relief and instantly recalled something Mark, a friend of mine, told me to tell pesky people. When someone is being a pain, you are supposed to say, "I'd like to help you out… which way did you come in?" I love that remark. I'm sure he stole it from somebody famous. He's such a plagiarist… but at least he doesn't have webbed feet.

There was also the guy who had been practicing for his best friend's bachelor party a little ahead of schedule. He came in and started rubbing my shoulders as I had my head under his schnauzer (dog). "I came to pick up Buddy," he said in a slightly slurred speech.

"I think it would be best if you didn't do that," I told him bluntly.

"Oh, yeah?' he said, leaning his head against mine. "And why do you think that?" he whispered loudly. The words never even got a chance to come out of my mouth before his wife's head appeared on the other side of his.

"Because your wife might not like it!" she yelled loud enough to wake every dead person in the Tri-state area. "I told you I was picking up the dog, you fool," she said, shoving a bony finger into his chest.

"Now, that's entertainment," I thought to myself.

So, you see, no matter where you are, no matter what you do, there are odd folks out there to put the moves on you! (Sorry, felt the need to rhyme there!)

Chapter 33

The Stray

You cannot work in the animal world and not have the weakness. You may be one of the lucky ones, but eventually enough moons will pass through your lifetime and you will have to make the decision. Yes or No… No or Yes??? Do you take the stray dog home or leave it to some other "Good Samaritan?" As you see the undoubtedly flea-infested, non-vaccinated, more bones sticking out than a runway model, probably more ill-tempered than your Mother-in-law's mutt, you just know you have to do it. You pull your vehicle off to the side of the roadway and call the poor thing to you. Of course, it doesn't listen.

You cringe as it darts back and forth against traffic. Just

what you *really* need. To add to your feelings the fact that it will probably be your fault. You, who are trying to save this creature, will be responsible for its untimely demise somewhere on the yellow line in front of you. For some reason your in-laws' image flashes before your eyes (just kidding...).

You finally play this coaxing game long enough to get the little refugee to come to you. As you reach out for it, you suddenly realize how fast your reflexes really are. Your hand comes dangerously close to leaving its familiar connection to your wrist. Just because you have a hard time remembering where you left your husband in the mall, doesn't mean you have a death wish. It's not really *your* fault that you forgot that he came with you in the first place. You are just used to going yourself so much that it confused you. But I digress...

You get the animal talked into the lesser of the two evils... crawling into your warm vehicle that smells reminiscent of French fries and Big Macs or staying out in the first official downpour of the spring. He weighs his options carefully and decides you are the lucky recipient of his company. It just so happens that on his way into your van he takes the most direct route... via *your* seat. There he sits, a quivering mop, fully soaked to the skin, which is now being dried, courtesy of your driver's seat. As you reach for him to put him into the rear of the vehicle, the excess water from his body squirts out onto your seats (I don't mean the rain). Sigh...

You talk your new friend into taking up residence on the back seat and you hop into the driver's seat. You wonder somehow with the law of averages just how many fleas can jump from the average dog into your upholstery within any given amount of time.

With this in mind, you drive maniacally to get to your destination of home. Suddenly, the odor overwhelms you and you recognize it instantly. Obviously, your new friend didn't "go" before he got into the car. As you hold your breath a little longer than the human body was originally intended to, you wonder what possessed you to be a do-gooder this particular day. I am pondering if I should stop the car to clean up the mess now, or wait the remaining three miles 'til I get home. My cheek gets wet, as a giant string of dog spit is lovingly deposited onto it. My ankle mysteriously begins to itch…

I get home and carefully extricate myself from the vehicle, being careful not to let my new friend slip out behind me. I didn't go through all of this to let him get away now. I am going to find this beast a wonderful new home. I go into the house to get a slip lead. Upon my return, I find that I must locate the extra set of keys, as my new buddy has quite effectively hit the electric door locks. Twenty-seven minutes (and another pile of whatever he ate for breakfast) later I am sliding the lead over his head.

I put the dog in the mudroom while I go back to tend to my car. Armed with every upholstery cleaner east of Mexico, I tackle the job like a pro. It ain't pretty, though. At one point I think of just turning the hose on the inside of the whole thing, but decide that probably isn't in my best interest. I am ever so close to thinking this would be an ideal time to let the bank repossess the vehicle, though. After more than an hour, the car is finally clean (well, passable, anyhow). Clean is a relative term, you know.

I go to the house to check on the dog and find that the door we used to have on the mudroom is not quite as I remember it. It seems less substantial somehow. It is now made into a Dutch door. Dog is having a ball, running through the basement, spreading piles of laundry everywhere. It could be worse, I guess.

I pick up the laundry and get rid of the extra "Mementos" that pooch has made for me. What some of them had originally been I don't know and probably don't want to know.

I reach down and extricate the dog's front legs from my calf, and decide that chances are quite good that he probably *is*, in fact, a male dog. I slip the lead over his head and head for the exit. As I crack the door open, I suddenly am propelled forward and down the outside steps. When his seventy or so pounds hit the driveway, I decide my first two fingers would be better left on the hand they have grown accustomed to after forty-two years. With that decision made in haste, I let go of the lead.

Off he heads down the driveway, through the field and across the road. I sigh, knowing there is nothing left for me to do to aid him. I feel bad. He seemed to be a nice enough dog personally. However, he was a tad destructive I felt.

Days passed, and one morning about 9:00 a.m., one of my girlfriends called me. "You'll never guess what I found," Maryanne was saying.

"Oh?" I said half questioningly.

"I was out hanging clothes and this big dog appeared out of nowhere," she was saying. "I put him in the extra bedroom downstairs last night, and I'm just getting ready to go say good morning to him."

I wonder if I could get a discount on interior doors if I were to buy two instead of one. I just have a feeling…

Chapter 34

Resumes

"Loyal, trustworthy, obedient...
Just what we're looking for."

I am not looking for any employees. The phone here rings several times a week with someone looking for a job with animals. Because, as they all tell me, "I just love playing with dogs." Yup. Playing. That's what we do as groomers. Right after they phone (they *always* phone first), they usually follow up with a resume. Even though I have politely told them I'm not in need of anyone, they feel I will surely change my mind when I see their impressive list of qualifications.

As I sit here writing this, I am flipping through a few of these resumes that I most recently received. Here's a good one. "Jill" is twenty-six. Okay there… She is planning to get her GED in the future sometime… right now isn't a good time though, as she is busy helping plan her sister's wedding. Not so okay there. She's got a car, but recently lost her driver's license to a DUI mix-up. When the trial's over, give me a call…

Here is one for "Ann." Ann's chief claim to fame at this point has been watching a lot of Animal Planet, so she feels pretty qualified to start into a "real job." She doesn't mention how many hours of AP she has under her belt at this point, but it sure sounds promising to me.

I really like "Julie's" resume, though. She, like Jill, did not graduate from high school. She contemplated getting a GED, but decided against it. Her exact words are as follows: "I wasn't never much for learning from books. I am what I call a realer. Somebody who learns about life stuff from really living all the time. I just don't think a GED would prove nothin'."

Oh, Julie, you have certainly proved something to me about not having finished that education…

To Julie's credit, under work experience she lists the following: "I helped my boyfriend rebuild the engine on his Camaro. It was hard. It took a lot of knowledge to get the pieces to fit together again." This was the most impressive thing Julie had to say on her resume.

Under the heading of references, she just said, "Feel free to talk to anybody that knows me. They'll tell you how nice I am." (Yeh, I thought so, too…)

One lady and her daughter thought that they would double-team me recently. The lady owns a Golden Retriever that I have been grooming for the last three years. So, one day the daughter calls anonymously and asks if I'm hiring.

"Sorry," I told her. "Not at this time."

The next day the mother comes in. "Pat is graduating from college this spring and decided she'd rather clip dogs," the woman said. "I thought I'd come in and pick your brain on this stuff," she was saying. "I mean, can you really make a living doing this sort of thing, or are you just in it for the fun? I know you really charge a lot to do *my* dog, but do you have enough business to make a living?

I'm not sure if you could handle competition from another groomer like my daughter. She's graduating from college this spring," she added again.

"Yes, you did mention her impending graduation," I told her while busily clenching my teeth.

"Are there any places where she could learn for a couple hundred bucks?" she asked.

"Maybe...," I replied, "if you don't mind working on cadavers."

It wasn't really a word that she uttered. More of an "ugh" with the added bonus of an eye roll. I could tell she thought that I was just being snide (She was right. I didn't even go to college to learn how to do it!). I politely informed her of an excellent school in the state, but that wasn't what she wanted to hear. She felt it would be better if I would let her daughter come to observe my grooming skills for "a couple days... just long enough to be able to start her own business on the right foot."

"Lady," I thought to myself, "your would need to be a centipede to have enough feet to stand on to learn this job in 'a couple days.'"

"Well, you just aren't going to be of much help with this, are you?" she asked after another twenty or so minutes had passed. I had controlled my temper completely during this time, but now wanted to make this lady turn into a fire hydrant right outside my door. Ya know?

8:04 a.m. the next day... "Yes, I'd like to know if you are hiring," a vaguely familiar voice says from the other end of the phone line. "I'm graduating from college this spring and..."

Chapter 35

The Land of Mispronounced Dog Names

"What breed? Gee, I'm not even sure whether it's a dog or not."

In a land of mispronounced dog breeds, I would have to vote the Lhasa Apso as the single most mutilated word. You *all* know what I mean, so don't be going "Huh?" The typical call in my place goes something like this…

Phone rings…
Me: Wonders Sassy Pup
Them: Is this the dog place?
Me: Yes, it is.
Them: Do you wash dogs?
Me: Yes, we do.
Them: Do you groom them?
Me: Yeeessss.
Them: I have a registered white dog. It needs a haircut or something.
Me: We can take care of that for you. What kind of dog is it?
Them: How much do you charge?
Me: It depends on the dog. There are so many different breeds and haircuts and grooming time can vary by a few hours for each dog. What kind of dog do you have?
Them: It's registered.
Me: You mentioned that before. What breed of dog do you have?
Them: It's a Lampampasomsis.
Me: A Lhasa Apso?
Them: Yeah… a Lasasisasis.

You, as a fellow groomer, know of what I speak. The dreaded "I have a dog, but know not what it is" customer. I have heard more mispronunciations of this poor beast than I could possibly recall.

One lady calls hers a Lampropis Ampso. I have tried to teach her how to say it correctly for nine years now. You would think I would have given up. My friends who know me quite well understand that I have a terrible penchant for those who massacre the English language.

My high school teachers would have been proud. However, I hasten to add that it is my 11th grade English teacher, who calls her dog a "Hassa Assa." She, at least, is close.

A guy walked in one day and announced that he was referred to me by his neighbor who owns "one of those Aspasis dogs. You know, the one that looks like somebody smacked him in the mouth."

Joe walked in with his pooch under his arm and stepped into the grooming room. A Shih Tzu sat upon my table, almost finished.

"Hey! That's the kind of dog my brother has," he exclaimed. "A Lappa Appa, isn't it?" he questioned.

I laughed. "Actually, it's a Shih Tzu."

"A what-zoo?" he asked, putting his hand to his ear.

"Shih Tzu," I pronounced again.

"Are you sure? It really looks like my brother's Lappa Appa," Joe insisted.

"It's a Lhasa Apso," I gently corrected him. Poor Joe. He was really confused now.

"I thought you just said it was something from a zoo."

"It's not from a zoo. It's called a Shih Tzu. Your brother's dog is a Lhasa Apso," I clarified for him.

"Does he bring it here for a bath, too?" Joe looked surprised. "I've been telling him he needs to have you bathe it sometime for him," he said.

"No, I haven't seen your brother's dog," I said, trying to keep from laughing at the whole episode.

"Then how do you know it's a Lappa Appa?" he queried, looking suspiciously at me.

"You just told me that two minutes ago," I said, defensively.

"Ugh," was his reply.

As he started toward the front door, another customer came in with a dog in her arms.

"Well, hello there, little dog," Joe said, as he lightly patted him on the top of the noggin'. "And what kind of dog are you?" he asked of the pooch.

"Mitzi is a Bichon," Wendy, her owner, told him.

Joe just sighed for a moment. I saw his hand go to his ear once again. "A what's that you say?"

"A BICHON," Wendy said, louder this time.

"In my day, a dog was a dog. I don't know when they started coming up with all these fancy names. Looks like a Poodle to me. But you came to the right place. She's got some kind of circus dog in the back there. She claims it came from a zoo. Imagine that!"

Yup… imagine!

Chapter 36

Sisters

"Sigh... The customer is always right!"

I would imagine that most of us have a spare one lying around somewhere. They are sometimes kind, sometimes thoughtful, sometimes precious... and sometimes none of the above. They can be used as a measure of your own intelligence, or lack of it.

I have one, and she has a dog. Lucky for me! I get the honor of grooming it. Now, you would think that having *me* as a sister would make her fly right when it comes to taking care of her dog's hair. Not so. In fact, a lesson could be learned just from watching her actions regarding her *own* hair.

This is typical Maryanne. First off, understand her own hair is short. I mean like Liza Minelli short. She constantly makes hair appointments for herself about every three weeks. She doesn't quite understand the concept that human hair grows only about 1/2 inch each month. So, how could she need one inch cut off every three weeks. Get my drift? It's not bad enough that she has these poor beauticians do this to her head, but then she does the ultimate...

She goes home, decides it's crooked or something, then "fixes" it herself. Then she cries about how "bad" the beautician messed it up. I mean the last time she had it done she actually told me she sat in her bedroom one morning and took a pair of scissors to her head because it had "too much bulk."

Yeah, I know some of you are thinking, "So what? We've all tried to trim our own hair!" Okay, you're right... but we at least do it in front of a mirror. Maryanne just sat up in bed, held out chunks of hair and started chopping. No mirror. Then she came in here to whine about what she had done. Yeah, it looked that bad. She scares me.

At any rate, you can just picture what she does to her dog. She owns a Shih Tzu. "Joey" is named after our brother, to whom she was pretty close. This dog is truly cute. A whiney cry baby that at the tender age of five still isn't quite housebroken. But he *is* cute.

As with most Shih Tzu owners in this area, my sister and her hubby like Joey cut with a #3 comb and his face and head scissored into a slightly longer round cut. The hair is trimmed out between the eyes. You know the look. My sister *thinks* she knows the look. That's where the problem starts... and usually has no end.

My brother-in-law brings the dog in. Just before he arrives, Maryanne calls and tells me how to cut him this time (It always turns out to be the exact same thing I do every time). Her main request is that his "manhood" be concealed, as he truly is exceptionally "gifted" in that area. I must agree with her there. Therefore, he gets a skirt to hide "things."

She tells me these things like I haven't already been doing this for the past five years. Then my brother-in-law leaves me with these specific instructions. "I know that Maryanne called you before I got here. Just do it like you always do," he tells me. I give him the thumbs up and bend down to pick up the dog. As I look into his little face, I see he is devoid of all hair from where he would have eyebrows, back to the front of his ears. He beard is forked like the devil's.

"What happened to him?" I yell as Bill is headed out the door.

"Your sister happened to him," Bill shot back as he made a hasty retreat.

My chest is heavy (and it isn't from my cleavage). I sigh. Why do people do this? I know they say it's because the dog couldn't see. I know most people want to see their dog's eyes. I know it's healthier for them not to have hair sticking up to scratch their corneas. *However...* What these people do in the name of "shaping up" their pets is criminal. My sister is the ultimate. She should stick to what she is good at. Not that I have any idea of what that might be, but there has to be something other than making a mess of perfectly fine human and animal haircuts. I don't mess with trying to be a fashion model. I mean, I know my limits. (Not that Ralph Lauren and his sidekicks don't call me constantly for this kind of stuff.) But, come on.

I call my sister. "What did you do to Joey?" I question.

"What? I didn't do anything. What's wrong with him?" she asks.

"You mean beside the fact that you made his face look like a gopher?" I reply. "Why can't you just keep your hands off this poor guy's face? He looks like Foo Man Chu or something!" I yell.

"You just said he looked like a gopher," she said, tartly.

"Oh, you know what I mean. You have this hair fetish. You just can't stand to let well enough alone," I scolded her.

"I was just trying to straighten it out," she said. "Hair was in his eyes." I knew I was going to lose this battle, as always.

"You cut it far enough back that it'll take two months to get enough back to make round again. What'd you do, use a Bic shaver on him?" I asked, smartly.

"Don't be stupid," she said. "It was an Epilady."

"MARYANNE!" I shouted.

"Oh, calm down. It was a disposable razor. Are you happy? You know I *am* your sister. Your elder. You treat me like a child sometimes. You should treat me with respect if for no other reason than I am older than you," she admonished. "Besides, he is my dog," she reminded me.

This is true, and we all have to do whatever the customer tells us to.

"Yes, but when you whack him like this and people see him, they think I did it!" I defended myself. "I mean when people see *your* hair, what do you imagine they think about *your* hairdresser?" There was silence on the other end. I had her now.

"I tell them I'm a sixty-one year old bag lady, who is your sister, but you won't cut my dog's hair, so I do it myself. Happy now?" she snickered. "I don't tell them who cuts his hair. I only tell them that we are sisters," she added.

I guess this was supposed to make me feel better.

I suddenly recalled a few weeks ago when two of my customers were in the shop at the same time shooting the breeze as I finished their dogs.

"Have you seen her hair lately?" one lady asked the other.

"No, but I saw her dog's," the other replied.

"It's a shame. They both look like trolls. Who would think her own family would be like that?" the other responded.

Could they have been talking about?... Nah!!!... Still...

Chapter 37

Wrong Door

"I knew you'd be back!"

Tuesday morning the front door of my shop burst open, and as I came around the corner, I was in time to see a woman hurl a little kid at me.

"Just cut his bangs. Let the rest go right now. I'll be back in a minute," she said, all out of breath.

With that, she was out the door in a flash, and there stood this five year old looking at me with his hands on his hips.

"Where's the stickers?" he demanded. I was so dumbfounded by this whole episode that all I could manage was, "Huh?"

He looked at me with about as much irritation as a Chow-Chow when you are trying to get the grooming noose over its no-necked body.

"Stickers." He was cut short by this same woman again, flinging the door open. I, at this point was assuming it was his mother or a really dumb child-napper.

"Wrong door," she puffed at me, thrusting a Terrier-looking thing into my arms. At the same time, she spun the kid around and grabbed him around the waist, and I thought for sure he was going to be airborne for a minute. This was one powerful lady!

"Do you still want just the bangs cut on this one?" I asked, comically.

"Don't get cute," the lady said. "I'll be right back... again," she added.

I knew exactly what had happened in this instant. You see, my shop is in a long building with a couple of hairdressers next door. Many times someone has dragged a canine companion into the "Hair Girls'" place, as we affectionately call them. I love the look of embarrassment on a customers' faces when they realize what they've done. I don't think the girls next door like it very much when Fido gets scared as his owner tries to pull him out their door, and he lets loose with his bladder. Yeah, I'm hateful. On the other hand, I've had my share of *their* scary-looking customers come into my place, looking for some body part to be waxed... or whacked!

Don't get me wrong. I have the utmost respect for anyone who wants to deal with people for hours at a time. I mean there are definite similarities between our clientele. Take a screaming kid in for its first haircut. I've seen it happen when I have been having my own hair cut. Parents bring in kid. Kid realizes he's been brought in as a sacrificial cow or goat or something, and for all he knows is about to be beheaded. Parents are standing there so *proud* of the little tyke, getting his first trim. Out pops the camera from Mom's purse, and Dad is looking right over her shoulder with a camcorder glued to his eyeball. Meanwhile, the poor hairdresser is trying to get the cape on the kid, who likens it to a straight jacket when she fastens the gown around his neck.

Mom and Dad are cooing at the rug rat that it's "O.K. Don't be scared," they are saying, as he now turns six shades of blue from screaming so hard. All the while, the flash keeps blinding *me,* and I realize that I am in direct line of fire for that stupid camera. How many shots they will have of me with my long wet bangs combed down over my face. I know at this point I look like "Cousin It." Yeah, I'm mortified.

As I sit there, I think to myself it's the same situation dog groomers face when it comes to puppy's first hair cut. As we all know, it is usually pretty uneventful after the first couple minutes. If, however, we allowed every parent to stay when this was occurring, you know utter chaos would ensue. I have been moaned at, whined at and cussed at for not allowing owners to stay for the grooming process.

I could teach those hairdressers a thing or two about retaining control of their establishments. I would, of course be tactful. I would probably say something like this... "Of course, you're welcome to stay while Johnny gets his first haircut. However, if he poops in my chair, upchucks his breakfast on my floor, bites me in the elbow while I'm scissoring his bangs, or God forbid, widdles all over his feet, you'll have to clean it up. Here's a roll of paper towels and baggies... just in case." Pretty much works every time.

Chapter 38

Are We Having Fun Yet?

People become famous for different reasons. Some are great baseball players. Some are wonderful singers. Some lead the country in times of battle, and some are dog groomers with extraordinary talent. I, of course, don't fall into any of the afformentioned categories. I don't consider myself any more gifted than most when it comes to grooming. I *do*, however, bring the gift of gab to the profession.

My customers come in for grooming but usually get to know my place is one of mirth. I figure if a customer can't handle my brand of humor, then there are other places who will love their business. Life is far too short to be cranky. Take, for instance, my signage. The latest sign in the shop was born from necessity. I had a customer who decided to tell me that he wasn't pleased with the last grooming his dog received. Now, I know that I certainly could have been having an off day, could have been trying to squeeze too much into too few hours, or just, in general, screwed up. *However*… this guy has been coming to me for fourteen years now, and for about thirteen of those years, he has a different gripe each time.

He came in on a Tuesday morning at 7:30 a.m. I saw him coming and opened the main door for him. As I smiled and said, "Hi, there," he thrust the Lhasa into my chest.

"You really screwed him up last time you gave him his haircut," he boomed.

Not really ready for this first thing in the morning, I was dumbfounded, so all I could say was, "Huh?"

"You screwed him up bad. One side of his leg was cut clean off! He had a big bald spot right in front. I tell you, Missy, you better straighten up, or I'll be taking my business elsewhere!" he threatened.

"I'm so sorry if I did something wrong," I flubbered. "Where was it?" I asked worriedly.

"Right here," the guy pointed out. There was an obvious patch of hair missing from a right front leg. It was pretty apparent that the leg had been shaved a few weeks ago for an IV or a blood draw.

"Did you have him to the Vet for anything lately?" I asked with a frown.

"Yeah, he had the craps for a couple days, and he had to go to the hospital for awhile. How'd you know?" he questioned.

"I didn't screw him up… The Vet shaved this for an IV or something," I explained, heaving a sigh of relief.

"Yeah? Well, don't *you* screw it up, anyhow! Give him a good haircut!" he said, huffily, as he slammed the door.

"No, I'm gonna give him the *worst* haircut in the world, you old crank!" I yelled back at him. "I'm gonna shave him buck naked and neuter him for you while I'm at it." Okay… well, I didn't *really* say any of that. But I *wanted* to. Come on, you know you'd have had the same urge.

At any rate, that made me put up a new sign in the shop that day. It reads, "THIS IS A HAPPY PLACE WITH HAPPY PEOPLE. $20 SURCHARGE IF YOU CHANGE THAT!"

You wouldn't believe the look on people's faces when they come in and read that. First, it's a look of concern. Then the meaning of it registers. Then *everybody* laughs because they know exactly what it means. I've had more cute comments from customers, and since that sign appeared, I haven't had to deal with any other crotchety persons. I'm biding my time on Mr. Crank.

I admit I think I have the nicest customer base around. I've long ago gotten rid of the majority of sourpusses. Most everybody who comes in gets a hug by the time they leave.

The older gents really get a kick out of it. We joke a lot in the shop, and one elderly guy makes a point of telling us he still bowls at age 81, and his teeth are real. That revelation came one day when Lou took her smock off as she was leaving, and he showed his appreciation for the T-shirt that she was wearing.

"My, oh my! What a babe you are!" he exclaimed. "These are my own teeth, and I can dance, too," he revealed.

I thought I would bust a gut laughing so hard. Lou, on the other hand, was not sure how to respond, so all she uttered was, "That's ahhhhh… good!" She looked at me, and I was leaning on the grooming table, trying to regain my composure. I couldn't!

"You know, I get the best entertainment of all my years in this place," the guy said. "And the best part is, I don't have to pay for it. My son foots the bill for the dog, and I get to be the delivery boy. It's like *Pizza Hut*, and you girls are the pepperoni on my pizza!" We absolutely howled.

One guy, who is 92 years of age, I believe, comes in every month with his dog. "You know, the little guy really doesn't need a haircut right now," he often says. "I just come in for a hug. But, since I brought him along, go ahead," he says with a smile. Then, he always says the same thing as he hands me the leash… "you can hug me now." I get such a kick out of him! When he comes to pick the dog up, the process is repeated as he takes the animal from me.

I go through my share of trying to be matchmaker for customers, too. I have *yet* to be successful. I think I scared one guy to death, just last week. I have an extremely close friend who is looking for Mrs. Right, and I try my best to match him up.

So far, I have managed to fix him up with a lady who confessed to him that she is a witch (but the good kind, or so she says). Next was a woman who was married, and just wanted to make her husband jealous to see if he would literally fight for her. And my last pick was a woman who thinks she may have been born a man, but I guess the verdict isn't in on that one yet. I don't know how I do this stuff… It just happens.

No, it has never occurred to me to just stick to grooming dogs. I actually have too much fun with my customers to just groom their dogs. So, if you are ever in the area, stop in and I will be glad to teach you about having fun in this business. And, if you're looking for a nice guy, Mark is still available as of this writing…

Chapter 39

One Mistake Reaps Much Regret!

I am going to 'fess up to something that I never thought I would admit to anyone, much less the majority of the dog grooming world. About fourteen years ago, I broke one of the cardinal rules of the profession: Never let a customer stay with you while their dog is being groomed. Yes, I will own up to the fact that I made an exception in one lady's case, and I rue the day I allowed it. Now, after many moons have passed, and so has one of her dogs, I am still searching for a way to tactfully get her out of my grooming room.

This lady, whom we shall call Ann, has steadfastly refused to leave her animals totally in my care whilst they are being groomed. In the beginning, when I was hungry for business (and an occasional *Big Mac*) I let her talk me into letting her stay for the first grooming.

In my defense, her dogs did not behave badly at all while she stayed. Therefore, I could not use the excuse that misbehavior would ensue if she didn't leave me alone with them. She chatted incessantly the whole time she was there, and sometimes her stories were rather entertaining. It wasn't necessarily her constant chatter, much akin to what squirrels look like when they are bickering with one another, but rather her preoccupation with cleaning up my grooming area that got on my nerves. I mean this is a woman who owns five vehicles that each look like they did when they rolled off the showroom floor. Never mind that the newest one is more than eight years old! White interior, to boot, and not a speck of dirt anywhere on it.

This lady has eighteen barn cats, and they have litter boxes in the barn. There is also a good deal of carpeting in her barn. I don't know how many of you understand the concept of a real barn and its purpose in life, but people just don't put that kind of stuff in them. At least, not to actually use in there. However, she does. You should be getting an idea of what I'm up against at this point…

So, there we are, Lou and I, knowing full well that Ann will be thirty minutes early for her appointment. True to form, she arrives for her 11:00 a.m. at 10:29.

However, we are prepared for this event. Lou readies the dog for its bath, with Ann standing at her side at the bathtub, ready to give either the dog or Lou CPR if necessary, for some unforeseen reason. Along with Ann's instruction not to get water in the dog's eyes, nose, mouth or ears, Lou gives me a look that is obviously questioning me if she could perhaps slip Ann's head under water. I give a smile. I have to be sympathetic as I know my turn will be coming up shortly.

Lou adds the shampoo to the tub, turns on the HydroSurge and creates a two tablespoon splash of water outside tub. Immediately, Ann is on this one. Grabbing a sponge she is sopping up the water and waiting with what reminds me of batter-like stance for more water to spout from the tub. Lou, being the consummate professional she is, has it totally under control. I am mentally tallying up the cost of the eighteen paper towels that Ann has under her armpit.

I look over from the dog that I am grooming to see Lou beginning to rinse Sparky. In the same instant, Ann is over at the end of the tub twirling her finger over the drain to collect any hair that will be caught in the trap. I see her flinging what looks to me like imaginary hair follicles into the trash can. I keep quiet, my heart feeling heavy for what Lou is going through.

As she finishes toweling off the dog, Ann is making sure that she positions herself akin to a human barricade in front of the air conditioner (which is incidentally a mile and a half away from the dog) so as not to get him chilled.

Meanwhile, I am panting like crazy, as she is blocking the cool air from coming my way. I grit my teeth very quietly.

There are few times during the course of a month that I am thankful for the noise created by the airflow of the big force dryer. However, now is one of those times. Lou turns it on slowly, and Ann starts talking again. Lou is nodding in agreement at nothing in particular that Ann is complaining about and starts inching the variable speed knob up. Soon it is impossible for any conversation to be heard over the noise. I see Lou lower her head and turn her eyes my way. She looks at me with a crooked smile like someone who has had a stroke. I understand.

Just before the dog is dry, in walks my sister (the nutty one) with her husband. I let Maryanne know that the wooden train planter I had ordered for her has arrived. Her husband, Bill, promptly opens the boxes and starts to assemble it on the floor next to my grooming table. Now, I have Ann directly in front of me at the head of the table, her dog on my table, my sister on my left, and my brother-in-law at my feet. I reach for my clipper and nearly get my wrist broken as I learn Bill is accidentally sitting on the cord.

"Could you move?" I ask him.

"Uh-huh," he says, smiling and nodding. Meanwhile, he is not moving.

"Would you move?" I repeat.

"Ha ha," he chuckles this time. I should mention that he desperately needs a hearing aid at the tender age of 68. Knowing he didn't hear me either time, I give one mighty unmerciful yank on the cork, which probably gave him cord-burn on his skinny little rear. "Ohhhh," he exclaims, wide-eyed. I heave a heavy sigh.

As I begin clipping, my sister is holding her own with keeping Ann occupied in conversation, which helps free me up from any incessant behavior.

"What a beautiful little dog," Maryanne is saying. "I have one that looks identical to him!"

"Oh, really?" I hear Ann respond.

"Yes," Maryanne says. "What breed is he?" I almost drop my clipper.

"He's a Shih-Tzu, you goon," I say "You just told her he looks just like your dog. Don't you know what you have by now?" I shook my head. And she wonders why I try to keep it under wraps that we're related!

Even through all the commotion with Bill swearing because he can't find the screws that were to be included in the train kit, Maryanne telling Ann all about her dog's preoccupation with the toilet bowl, and me trying to keep my cord out from under Bill's derriere, it still happens. Ann is able to systematically pick up each tuft of dog hair that the suction system misses. Nary a hair will hit the floor with that woman around.

I clean up pretty much as I go, but this woman is insane. I pick up a brush, and before I can put it down, she's got it swiped clean of any hair. The same goes for any comb. When it comes to scissors, she towels them off before they can hit the table. She always takes one of the spare Clipper Vac hoses and vacuums as far as she can possibly reach. She would be wicked in a dentist's office with one of those spit-sucker things.

I have gone down this road with this woman for so many years that I should be used to it by now. I know it's my own fault that I let it happen, but the way I see it, I am making somebody really happy because nobody else would put up with this. After all, it's really not that bad.

My sister called today. "I got you a new customer," she was saying.

"Oh, yeah?" I said without much concern.

"Yeah, she was complaining because she would like to stay while her Old English Sheepdogs are being groomed, but her groomer won't let her. I told her you wouldn't mind at all!"

"Maryanne!!!" I exploded like Mount St. Bonnie, but not very "saintly" after all.

"W-h-a-t?" she was whining… "What did I do now?"

That's it. She's officially out of the will for this one…

Chapter 40

Treats Sometimes Save the Day!

"It's always a dog day afternoon around here."

Yesterday started out just fine... until the German Shepherd walked into the door. You might be thinking I meant *through* the door. No! I mean *into* the door. All 132 pounds of him. You can't imagine the size of the dent he left in the storm door. There he was... standing calmly by his owner's side in the shop while she was paying his grooming bill. Suddenly Mrs. Kessler was on her way to the storm door to enter the shop when Bo (the Shepherd) got wind of her Yorkie, Pixie, in her arms. *BAM* went that hulk of canine masculinity as he tried to pull a Casper and pass magically through the front door.

Poor Mrs. Kessler and Pixie. I don't know if it was from the sheer sound of his body hitting the aluminum door or the reverberation, which was probably felt all the way up North Center Avenue. At any rate, the sight of that not so petite lady (if you get my drift) and the two-pound dog that was buried in the woman's arm making a mad dash for the car was a true *Kodak* moment. Then there was the surreal vision of the Shepherd's owner doing what I've seen *WWF* participants do to each other in the ring. The splat of when she dove onto her dog and hit the tile floor was unnerving. She could have been a contender, I tell you. I winced in sympathy for her pain. That move had ibuprofen written all over it.

The hulk of a dog looked kind of "taken aback" (I have always wanted to use that word somewhere). Anyhow, I didn't know if I should be grabbing for the dog who was now carrying on like he was plugged into a 220 outlet, or try to extricate his owner from beneath the vanilla cow ear bin that she rolled under when tackling her dog. Sometimes you just gotta go with your gut feeling… ya know? I chose to help Mrs. Marker to her feet. "Are you okay?" I was asking as I pulled a cow ear from her head. She was looking rather sheepish at that moment. (Or should I say "cowish?" Ha ha.)

"Just get my Bobo," she was begging me. She waived my help, as she unceremoniously dragged herself to the corner by the door. She put her arm on the display shelf and let her head rest on her forearm. "Just let me collect myself," she was saying. Meanwhile, I got Bo's leash and pulled the Tazmanian Devil's twin over to Mrs. Marker's side. I glanced up long enough to see what had become of Mrs. Kessler and Pixie. There she was, still in her car, clutching her dog to her bosom. At least I thought it was the dog she was holding. It occurred to me that it might have been her chest she was holding, and I had a fleeting thought that maybe I should call 911 in the event she was having a stroke or something from her fright. My place was quickly beginning to look like a trauma unit. "You're in good hands... with *Allstate*" was the tune that was playing in my head at that precise moment. I was thankful I remembered to keep up with my premiums.

"I feel so nauseous," Mrs. Marker was saying. She *was* looking rather peaked. "Did you hit your head?" I asked, alarmed. I don't know what I thought I was going to do if she had. I envisioned wrapping her head in a big white towel or something. I hadn't the foggiest notion what good that would do. It just seemed like a plan, I guess.

"I don't think so," she said. "I just smell an awful odor suddenly," she complained. "Makes me want to puke."

Oh, she was so graphic!

"What *is* that smell?" she demanded of me.

I looked where she was now sitting. "Uhh, you have your head next to the Pizzers," I told her.

"The what?" she asked, narrowing her eyes.

"Pizzers," I repeated.

"What on earth does that mean?" she asked with obvious irritation in her voice.

"They're Bull Pen****," I told her. I thought for sure she was going to pass out right then.

"Why would you have such a thing in here?" she demanded.

"They're treats. Dogs love them," I explained. Forget the passing out... she was *much* nearer the puke thing *now*. If nothing else, that made her get to her feet with greater speed than I would have imagined possible.

At least I learned one thing at that moment. If someone passes out and you have no smelling salts, you could always substitute one of those and the subliminal thought of what it is will awaken a squeamish victim.

"I think we are ready to go now," Mrs. M. said, as she straightened her shirt and picked up her purse and Bo's leash simultaneously. I checked out the front door and the Yorkie and her owner were still safely inside their vehicle.

"Make a break for it," I said, smiling as I held the door open for her. The two ladies gave each other nasty looks as Mrs. Marker passed Mrs. Kessler's car.

Sure… *now* Pixie was showing her stuff. All two pounds of her was bouncing off the inside of the rear car window at the German Shepherd. She looked like she had a spring attached to her rear the way she was *boing*-ing up and down after Bo. What a dreamer. I can still see that flopping bow in her topknot "wanging" this way and that way as she shot off her mouth… And Pixie's hair looked kinda out of control, too….

Chapter 41

Happy Holidays to One and All

Here we go again… another year of overbooking for the holidays. You know exactly how it goes. The customers start calling too near the impending party date, and you have no openings in which to squeeze dear "Muttley." Hence, the story goes…

The phone rings with a person pleading for an open appointment… "I'll take anything you have dear," they are saying. This is one of your better customers, so you make a concerned effort to accommodate.

"How about December 17th at 7:00 a.m.?" you offer.

"Are you kidding?" they say. "I couldn't possible be out of bed by then, much less to your store at that time!" they exclaim.

"But that's all I have, and even that is really rushing me at this late day," you say.

"Well, can't you do something else? Anything else?" they beg.

You scan the book... scanning... scanning... "Okay, I have 5:30 on Friday, December 13th," you try again.

"Friday, the 13th? I think not..." she says. "Besides, I have a nail appointment."

At this point you are really trying to contain the snippy remark that is right on that already inflamed taste bud on your tongue.

"You did say *anything*," you remind her. "I just don't have any open appointments at this time. If anyone cancels, I'll be glad to call you," you offer.

"Don't you think you could be a little more accommodating for my needs just this once?" she is asking. "After all, I have been a steady customer for the last six years," she reminds you.

Now you are cursing to yourself to find last year's "who gave you what" list from last Christmas. Finding it at last, you realize... yup, she was one of those "$25 and over" gifters.

I hear you... Say what you want about killing yourself at this time of year! Don't give the "money isn't everything" speech. Save that "you shouldn't make exceptions for people who don't have the sense to book early" lecture. In my book, as long as I keep getting letters in the mail from somebody named "Due by..." then Andrew Jackson speaks loud and clear to me. As do *JC Penney, Boscov's, Bon-Ton* and all their friends.

And then there's my gift list. I mean, Christmas at my place is more like Trick-or-Treating when it comes to the people in my building lining up for their gifts. They come one by one to my back door looking like lost puppies.

"Hi," they say on December 24th. "I just wanted to wish you a Merry Christmas," the guys say. They smile at me and linger a bit too long for just well wishes. I thank them, open the door and insert the annual envelope into their greedy little hands.

"Merry, Merry," I tell them. They thank me profusely.

They all have families with little kids, and they do help me out many times when I get deliveries that come on pallets and need a forklift to unload or major muscle to handle. They work for my landlord, not me, but sometimes I find the need to "borrow" them for just a sec or two.

However, as a friendly reminder to them, I yell out the back door as they are scurrying away… "My favorite store is *Victoria's Secret*… in case anybody is interested for my birthday or any other occasion."

Hey, I know it's shameless, but it actually did work for my birthday this year. Let me add, I made quite a haul, too.

So, there you are, back to trying to figure out an appointment to give this insistent customer.

"O.K., the only other time I can possibly get you in would be one or two on Tuesday, December 10," you give as a last attempt.

"Oh, that's perfect!" she says, surprising the crap right out of you. "I'll be there at 1:02."

"One o'clock *or* two o'clock," you clarify.

"Yes… silly me I see," she says. "Goodbye."

You hang up smiling after all. Another crisis averted in the land of dogdom. Again, the phone rings. "I need an appointment for December 23 or 24, and I prefer around 3:00 p.m., if possible," the voice on the other end of the line is saying to you.

However, that little voice in your head…

Happy Holidays!

Chapter 42

The Great Escape

I know this is supposed to be a story about the perils of pet grooming, but this time I just have to switch subjects. If it helps you adjust, just imagine that the animals involved are dogs… However, I have to admit they are horses (just think *big* dogs). I'll warn you now though… partial nudity is involved in this one. Yep, it's mine. And so the story goes…

There I am puttering around the house on a *very* snowy Sunday morning. Those of you who live in an area where it does snow will really appreciate this rendering. I glanced into a mirror on my way down the hall and noticed my roots really needed touching up. Of course, I am a totally natural blonde, but I just brighten up my shade a tad with the help of a box of Clairol (ahem). At any rate, I stripped and only put on an old bathrobe before I started the hair color process. There was no sense in using a good robe, for if you drip any color on clothing, you have totally ruined it. The one I use has a broken zipper and would do just fine. It was already marked for the garbage can, anyhow.

I mixed the hair color and applied it to my head. I hate this process. You nearly freeze while you walk around in the winter with your head soaked in peroxide glop for twenty-five minutes. But, I shouldn't complain. It's not like I had to wait out in the ice storm that was starting outside. Ugh, it was *such* a miserable day. The wind was whipping across the field behind the house and the ten or so inches of snow that had fallen the night before was drifting several feet high in the yard. It had been snowing all night, and with the wind picking up, you could barely see ten feet in front of you. I flicked through the channels on TV and couldn't find anything that I could get remotely interested in. I looked at the clock on the mantel. I had six more minutes to go, and then I could jump in the shower and rinse out my color.

I plodded lazily into the kitchen and leaned on the fridge. "Six minutes, six minutes," I was thinking. I glanced outside through the French doors. Suddenly I noticed the wind subside for just a second or two and my mouth fell open large enough to swallow a small crow.

There stood two of the horses in the aisle leading from the barn to the pastures. Directly in front of them was the gate to the outside world swung WIDE open. There I am looking at them. There they are looking at the gate, and then at each other. You can see the mice running through the wheels in their heads. "Hey… Freedom???" they are saying to one another. They were still in a position that I could run out there and swing that gate shut before they could go on their own version of The Incredible Journey. You have to understand that where we live, there are a gazillion acres of farmland all around us. Huge open fields that eventually lead to very dense woods and then to a major highway.

I instantly sprang through the house, stopping just long enough to jam my feet into a pair of winter boots. There was no time to zip them up… I needed to get out there before the impending disaster took place. I opened the door and the wind nearly knocked me on my not-so-elegant derriere. As I flew down the porch steps, I saw the horses were on their way through the gate and headed for the side field, which is not on our property. Rather, it belongs to a man who has a name that I'm not sure of. We just call him Crabby Farmer Guy. (*That*, in itself, is another story…)

Now, wouldn't you know that very morning I decided everybody's halters were really filthy and that I would throw every single one of them into the washer (their halters… not the horses). The horses see me coming, and I try to be nonchalant as I head for the barn to get some grain in a bucket. I use my head and don't run, as I don't want to spook them and have them start running. As I glance over at them, they… yeah… started running anyhow. That's what I get for using *my* head. I grab a bucket, fill it with sweet feed and yank two lead ropes off the wall. I go tearing out the front of the barn and turn right. Just about that time another gust of wind comes up and totally open goes my robe. I told you the zipper was broken. Now it is *really* broken. We have neighbors right across the road, but I was oblivious to any of that at that precise moment. You know how you get when you are afraid for your animals. Nothing else matters at that moment.

In hindsight, though, I can just imagine the scene as this fiasco plays out. It's 7 degrees out; my head is soaking wet with slimy coloring goop all over it; I am naked under a teal green robe with nothing to hold it shut but my hands, which are full of lead ropes and a feed bucket; my boots are trying to be sucked off my feet in the snow since I failed to zip them up; I have no socks on inside of boots, so my toes are freezing as I run back and forth, trying to capture either horse that at this point is enjoying the wind whipping through its mane as it savors the freedom. Both horses are trotting along rather nicely now. I slow to a calm walk in their direction. Yes, I am swearing. All the while my six minutes have long since passed, and I briefly wonder if I will have any hair left to color another time. I have now been outside about fifteen minutes, I am guessing.

Suddenly, by some really huge stroke of luck, one horse turns back toward me and spies the grain bucket in my hand. "Hmmmm," he says as he stops about ten feet in front of me. As any equine owner knows, this is the easiest way to catch one of these elusive creatures when they escape. Horse owners *also* know that their faithful steeds can extend their necks about thirteen feet out of their normal range of reach when there is food involved. They also have a rubber band mechanism in their neck that allows them to snatch a bite and retract their neck just in time to escape your hand going around their head.

I reach a tad forward with the bucket toward the horse. He reaches a tad forward toward the bucket. He thrusts his head deep into the bucket, and as I reach to lay the lead rope over his neck, I am plummeted with snow kicked up by the other horse as he zooms past us to check out the upper field. My robe is wide open, and I dare not move too quickly that I miss my chance at a capture. I see cars coming down the road, and I am in full view of them. "Why does this stuff *always* happen to me?" I wonder in amazement. My life is *so* full of Kodak moments! I hear someone honk a horn. Ahhh, it wasn't for me. I'm certain they were just honking at our neighbor or something.

I now have a horse that is oblivious to me and is content to be eating his extra brunch. I am able to get the rope all the way around his neck and lead him back to the barn. The other horse sees his friend leaving, and follows obediently behind. I get the first one into the barn. The second horse is half in and half out of the front barn door. I offer him the feed bucket, and find he is a true master of that rubber band technique. I am so tired and frozen from my jaunt through the field. "Oh, come on, Bud," I plead. I inch toward the door and he reaches again for the feed. He snatches a bite and taunts me to come outside. I play the game and step out a few paces into the snow. I am fast losing patience now and probably also my hair. He reaches for another bite, and I manage to get my hand close enough to grab a fistful of his mane. Here is a tip from someone who has been there… when you have a horse in full flight mode, and he spins and takes you down the driveway, and you are losing your open robe and one boot, LET GO! I tell you, it wasn't a pretty sight. I don't know *why* I insisted on hanging on. I mean he *does* outweigh me by about 1100 pounds. Needless to say, I lost the battle… along with a boot. I did, however, recapture the half of the robe that slid off my left arm.

Wouldn't it just figure then, that this horse decided he missed his friends too much to go on anymore, and he turned and headed into the barn on his own. I ran half-booted up the driveway and into the barn.

I put Bud into his stall and high-tailed it into the house, plucking my lonely boot out of the snow on my way there.

I flew in the front door and paused only long enough to look at the clock. I had been outside about twenty-four minutes. I have *never* had a shower that felt as good as that one did. On the plus side, I think I retained most of my hair. I didn't get frostbite, and I don't have pneumonia (yet). The strangest thing though is that since the episode, Crabby Farmer Guy has been waving and smiling at me every time I see him outside. Hmmmmm....

Chapter 43

At All Cost, Avoid the Flu!

I don't know about your neck of the woods, but here in Western Pennsylvania, the flu has been running rampant. I, however, know the importance of my annual flu shot, and the fact that if I can't work, there is no money brought into my humble establishment from grooming. Therefore, I faithfully get the shot each year, and the flu faithfully stays away from my doorstep… until this year.

It may have had something to do with the generic way I got my shot this year. I mean, I always go to my M.D.'s office, wait in one of the little white rooms, get the crabbiest nurse in the place, have her ask which arm I'd prefer to have it in, and then grit my teeth as she rams it into the opposite one. Yeah, I know I could correct her, but she's like Hitler in drag, so I don't irritate her any further.

I then pay my little co-pay and stay healthy for another year. This year I tried a different approach, however. Since I groom my doctor's dog, I thought it would not be that big a deal for him to just bring my shot to the grooming shop this year.

Doc had called for an appointment (yes, he actually calls for it himself and brings the dog in. No housekeeper, no teenage kid, and no maid… It always impresses me.) and Lou took the call. Just before she hung up, she looked at me and said, "I made it for Thursday. Is that okay with you?"

"Fine, but tell him since I give him his appointments at the drop of a hat, that the least he could do is to bring me my flu shot this year," I said loudly enough, of course, that I knew he would hear me.

"Did you catch that?" Lou asked him, grinning.

"Oh, yes, I caught that whole thing," he told her.

Lou hung up the phone and turned toward me. "You don't actually think he's going to bring it to you, do you?" she asked in disbelief.

"Nah, I just thought I'd razz him," I replied.

Thursday came, and lo and behold, in Doc walked with a manila folder, which held my chart stuff and a syringe.

"Bear it," he said with a smile. I offered my arm and the deed was done. Lou and I were both shocked that he came through. That is the last time I'll try that method, however, after this past weekend.

There I was, drifting in and out of sleep on *Super Bowl* Sunday. The only way that day would excite me is if it involved a huge tub of ice cream, so I chose to use it to be lazy. The phone rang, and it was Lou.

"I can't come to work for awhile," she was informing me. It appeared that she had once again donned her artificial fingernails, and had a slight mishap. Those things have been the root of more calamities in the shop. She is forever popping one off at the wrong moment. Once I found one in a Poodle's topknot as I was ready to hand the dog to its owner. Just at that precise moment, I snatched the dog back from the lady, claiming that I saw a stray hair that needed snipping. I plucked the "barely-there-pink" piece of plastic from the dog's head and handed it to Lou on my way down the hall. There have been other incidents, but right now her problem was that she jumped over her hubby to answer the phone while they were in bed and landed on her thumbnail. Apparently, the whole thing bent backward and she ended up in the ER. She is now missing her entire natural nail. I'll spare you the gory details, even though she didn't.

At any rate, I found myself without my little buddy for a week that was pretty well booked with large and two-person dogs. After hanging up with her, I decided I needed to get the appointment book and see whom I could rearrange to another week. As I stood up, I felt not-so-pleasant in my stomach. I have not up-chucked since I was a small child, and I had a sudden vivid recollection of what it feels like before it happens.

Darn, Lou! If she hadn't told me that "story" it wouldn't have made me sick. As a fellow groomer, you kind of get the idea that if we can express anal glands, and discuss what's for dinner that night, then this nail thing shouldn't have bothered me. I don't know why it got to me.

Later that night as I was pledging my dying vows to the toilet bowl in which I had stuck my head, I decided that I had succumbed to the flu. There I was with my pillow and quilt, lying with my back against the baseboard heater and my head wedged between the toilet and the wall, knowing I would never groom another dog, never extricate another "hump-happy" dog from my calf. I didn't care. I was in need of last rites at this point. I finally slept in that position on the bathroom floor.

The next day came and went without my knowing too much about its passing, as I was passed out on the couch during most of it, too weak to do anything that normal humans do. I decided to take off the following day which was Tuesday, a day I am normally open. I was still too woozy to be of much value. I will say now, that I don't ever recall taking off from work because of sickness. I have groomed with two ankles sprained at the same time, while standing on crutches, while having every illness and ache known to man... but couldn't bring myself to do it with this case of the flu.

So, there I am on Tuesday, lying on the couch... still. This is when I first realized my importance in the dog world. The phone rings. It was my husband calling from his work place.

"You'll never guess who just called me," he was saying.

"O.K., who?" I played along.

"Betty Cramer," he said. She is one of my first customers and has her definite good qualities. However, she has never mastered the fine art of not knowing everything that is going on at all times. In other words... she's a busybody. Like you wouldn't believe!

"She said she called the shop a couple times and all she gets is the machine. She wanted to know where you are and why you aren't there," he was chuckling. "I told her you have the flu," he finished. "Thank God she doesn't have our home number, or she'd be bugging me here," I sighed.

Thirty minutes or so after I hung up with Don, the phone rang again. It was Steve from the beer distributor next door.

"What is wrong with you?" he bellowed into the phone. "Here I was making out the deposit when my phone rings, and it's some Betty woman wanting to know if I'll go over to your place to see if you're there. She says she called you a couple times, and she gets the machine. She says she's worried that something's wrong. You know, I have my own customers to take care of.... Don't be expecting me to take care of yours too, now!" he said, pretending to be all huffy.

"Yeah, I know. She already called Don. He told her I was sick." We chatted a bit and then hung up. Dog people... Some of them are really wacky.

Another half hour or so went by and again my phone was ringing. Again it is Steve.

"Now what?' I asked.

"Your lady called again just now," he was saying. "She said I didn't have to worry about you, that she talked to your husband and he told her you were sick. She just wanted me to know in case I was worried about you or anything."

"I don't believe all this," I said. "All this just because I'm not in just one day?"

"One more thing, though," Steve was saying.

"What?" I was losing patience.

"She wanted to know if I knew if you could groom her dog this Friday," he asked.

"Huh?" was all that would come out of my mouth at that point.

"She said she called a couple times, but didn't want to leave a message, so she asked me to find out for her. I'm supposed to call her back," he said, mockingly.

"Go sell some beer, Stevie," was my response.

I went to work yesterday. It felt good to be back with the human race again. I was actually looking forward to the prospect of grooming a dog again. I went into my office machine. "You have forty-seven new messages," it announced. I sat with pencil in hand, ready to start writing. I took four messages right off the bat. Suddenly there was a series of hang-ups that seemingly lasted forever. I stopped the machine and picked up one of the phones that has caller ID. There it was… Betty Cramer's name and number appeared. In the little block that shows how many times she called was figure… 26. Twenty-six times the woman called! That was her "I called a couple times," confession to Steve and my husband. All these calls were made between 7:45 and 9:30 Tuesday morning. And you thought you were important…. P-L-L-E-A-S-E!!!!

Chapter 44

In the Beginning

The other day I was thinking back to how I first got started in the grooming profession. Almost twenty years ago, my husband received a job offer in Albuquerque, New Mexico. This was an easy decision, as far as he was concerned. He grew up on the western slope of Colorado and was used to the look and feel of the country out there. For me, it was culture shock. I had lived in Pennsylvania all my life and wasn't quite prepared for the lack of trees, grass and water. I used to think tumbleweeds were something they made up for effect in the old western movies. Not so, I discovered when we moved out there.

Additionally, when we first got there, we had to live in a trailer court for six weeks. This was another thing I had never done. I grew up in a rather large house with few neighbors, and suddenly I found myself surrounded by an odd group of people. Now don't come down on me for saying that. Let me explain that there was a guy who each day would come to the trailer asking for something different each time. Once it was pencils, another day a cigarette, and once for toilet paper. One day he wanted half of a canned pear. Now, admit that he was a little odd, OK?

Then there were the kids who used to throw eggs in the mailbox every day. The mailman would lie on the horn in his mail truck when he got to our place. It would get so hot out there, that the eggs would often literally fry themselves in the box. Actually, that was a good thing. The few times it was cooler, I had a *real* mess to clean up.

Then there were other oddities in the area, but I decided that since we had to move to a place that wasn't exactly what I had pictured on the maiden voyage, I would do my own thing. The first order of business was to get a dog. The first and probably only rule of the "Court" was that there were no dogs allowed. This, of course, meant that I had no logical choice but to get the biggest dog I could find on short notice. Hence came Max, the Airdale, into our lives.

This big gangly brute of a canine entered our lives and hearts with no grace, manners or diplomacy at all. He would plow you down each and every morning as he greeted you when you came out of the bedroom. My kids were five and six at the time and they quickly learned to plaster themselves up against the walls when he first saw them or anytime they came inside and he hadn't seen them for more than five minutes. He would pin them against the walls and slobber them to death with his exuberance.

As I had planned with my aquisition of Max, we were evicted from the trailer court for having a dog. As I was less than happy with my hubby at the time for moving us a kazillion miles away from my friends, family and *water*, this was my revenge.

I found us a house in Sante Fe, which is about fifty or so miles from Albuquerque. Although the climate didn't change, our living accommodations were *much* more to my liking. The house was beautiful, the neighbors were normal and I could have my dog.

One day I sat looking at Max and commented to my husband that I think they get some sort of a haircut or something, as Max was definitely in rough shape. I called to make an appointment at a groomer. On the appointed day, I spent a good deal of time chatting with the lady who owned the place. It just so happened that I was able to talk her into letting me apprentice for her. I was *so* impressed with the dogs she had groomed and how clean and quiet her place was. Her father had groomed for twenty some years, I believe, and she learned from him. She also had been grooming for twenty-plus years and was relieved to have the prospect of help. Oh, and help I did.

I remember vividly dematting Old English Sheepdogs that were completely felted over. It took me an entire day and those poor things endured it. After I would finally be able to get a comb all the way through them, she would shave the dog down with a #7. Horrified, I would be near tears. "Why do you make me comb all that out if you are going to shave it off anyhow?" I moaned one day. "It's such a waste of my time," I complained.

"Because… Number 1, I am the *boss*. Number 2, You are my apprentice. And Number 3, SO YOU LEARN TO RESPECT YOUR WORK!"

That was it. I never, ever complained again, and I am so thankful that she was so hard on me. After that episode, she really started teaching me the "art" of grooming. I was taught pretty darn well apparently, as I have done better than average over the years.

Max, however, was my main guinea pig. That Airedale sported more Poodle feet than most Poodles do in an entire lifetime. I was always practicing *something* on him. He had the most amazingly *thick* coat. I could give him a topknot that was to die for when he was in a "growth" stage. He taught me the fine art of a "Sweetheart Clip." He couldn't quite carry off a "Bikini Clip," though, as he tended to have thunder thighs. He gave a valiant effort.

We left Santa Fe after two years when Don was offered a job in Orlando, Florida. Anxious to return to surroundings that were more familiar, we headed back East. That dog could fill a Honda Civic like you wouldn't believe. Without a doubt, the most memorable moment during that trip was when the dog finally peed. Not being used to traveling so far, Max refused to "widdle" for over two days. He drank and drank and drank, though. We kept stopping at every rest stop to try to get him to go, with no luck. *Finally,* just as I was saying we needed to find a vet somewhere to see what was wrong with him, he started to pee and pee and PEE! Then we were at a 7-11 kind of place, and my husband, both kids and I were standing in the parking lot clapping and yelling like crazy.

"Goooood Boy! See how *nice* he pees!" I remember singing out. I was so relieved to see him relieved. People came out of the store to see what we were going crazy over and what a sight that must have been… four people going nuts because a dog is peeing. I hear ya!

We spent two years in Orlando, and I put many more fancy coiffures on that dog. A couple times, I even cut him to look like an Airedale. I know it was my fault he had such an identity crisis. I don't think he ever *did* know what breed he really was.

We moved back to Pennsylvania after Orlando, and I opened a shop here. That was in 1989, and in 1997, we lost Max. He was almost ten at the time and was the kindest, most willing participant for getting a new "do" than any dog I have owned since. I miss him most when I have to groom Petey or Cindy or Meagan, the Airedales.

I'm still waiting for the day when someone asks me to paint one's nails and give that familiar pom on the tail. Then I'll know Max sent him to me.

About the Author:
Bonnie Wonders Trent

Born and raised in Southwestern PA, I have always had a love for dogs. However, "back in *my* day," I didn't know anything of dogs being groomed. The closest thing to venturing into the world of haircutting was when as 8-year-olds, my cousin and I would take a pair of safety scissors to her Terrier Poodle mix, B.J. Thankfully, he would lie still for the whole process. Not that he really had much choice in the matter seeing as how Debbie would lie atop him like a wrestler waiting for the "Three count."

All through my school years, I enjoyed writing stories for both fun and to stay on the English teacher's good side. This apparently worked out well, as I didn't spend any time with my nose in a chalk drawn circle on the blackboard in that class. That was where I spent many a 50 minute session in math, history and geography.

After graduating from high school, I got married, had two kids and a subsequent divorce. I re-married, moved to Santa Fe, New Mexico for two years (due to my husband's vocation) and bought an Airedale named *Max*. It was upon his arrival to our home that I decided he didn't look like pictures I had seen of his "kinfolk."

"I think he's supposed to have a special kind of haircut," I mused to my husband.

Thus began my apprenticeship at a very well-respected grooming and kennel facility after relentlessly pestering the owner. I began as a brusher-bather and eventually a full-fledged "groomer." Two years later we moved to Orlando, Florida and I continued on my own with the job.

Two more years passed and we moved back to Pennsylvania and I attended a NDGAA testing for non-sporting breeds and became officially certified (with high scores even!).

My grooming career was really off and running, and I have been grooming in Pennsylvania in my own salons since 1989. During those years I have had many occurrences of mishaps, blunders, comedic moments, frustration and some days that really work both the muscles and the heartstrings.

I have been very fortunate, however, to be blessed with a successful business and the ability to relay some of these stories, albeit with a tad of exaggeration here and there, for you to enjoy.

Bonnie

GROOM
& KENNEL EXPO
WEST COAST PET INDUSTRY TRADE SHOW
Southern California
• Top Industry Speakers
• World Cup Grooming Games
• Exciting Seminars
• Add-On Programs
• Creative Grooming Spectacular
Every February
Nearly 100 Booths
W1604
GroomandKennelExpo.com
(717) 691-3388
info@barkleigh.com